# RADIOHEAD

## a visual documentary

www.chromedreams.co.uk

# CONTENTS

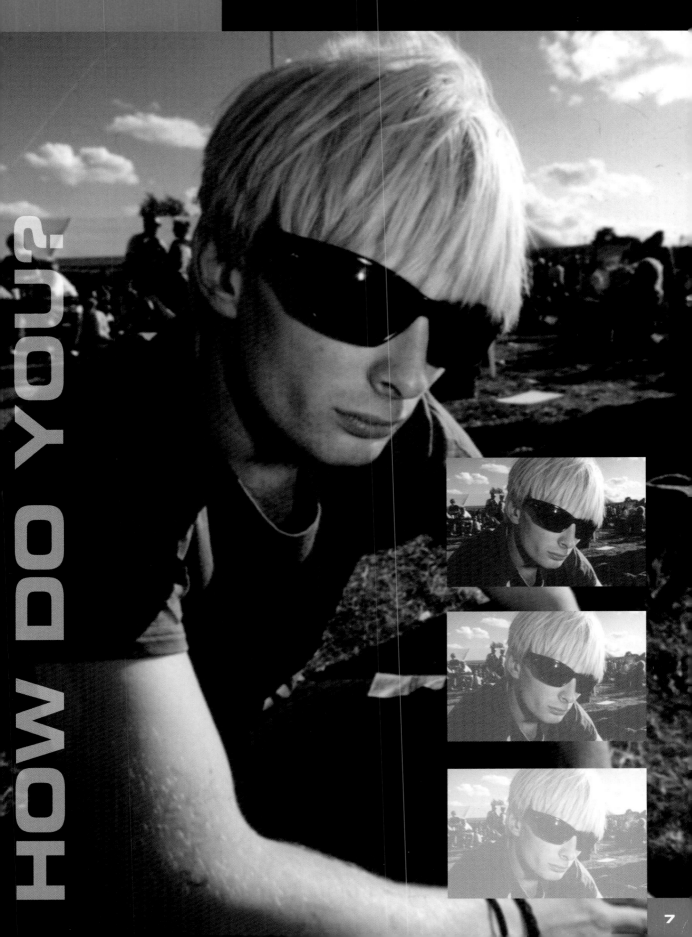

CHAPTER 1

HOW DO YOU?

# HOW DO YOU?

*"There's a certain state of mind I'm in when I write songs - it's like a bad virus."*
*Thom Yorke*

It's the 21st century. The musical scene has been smothered in a fluffy, marshmallow deluge of pure pop, and performers are simple-minded, blonde-brained puppets of producers and record company execs. Guitar music died when the third Oasis album came out (or was it when Jimi Hendrix died?) and the only interesting, innovative music is happening in underground clubs, for the enjoyment of half a dozen zealous fans.

Versace-clad stars are shunted from studio to gig to drying-out clinic in limousines with blacked-out windows and only hide the smack and groupies on top of the wardrobe when they do the photo-shoot with *Hello!* magazine. Then they try to prove their artistic credibility by doing something a little different, and fall on their now-saggy arses.

Well, that's how it feels sometimes. But the facts don't always bear it out. Because, in a universe of nu-metal, handbag garage and charideeee singles, a band turns up that can combine challenging, involving, compulsive music with the sort of commercial appeal that keeps the industry bosses in handmade cowboy boots for years. A band that can synthesise the progressive rock of Pink Floyd, the free jazz of Ornette Coleman and the twisted dance grooves of the Aphex Twin and transport the resulting astringent cocktail to the top of the US charts. A band that can collaborate with artists as diverse as PJ Harvey, DJ Shadow and Humphrey Lyttleton. A band that can communicate profound ideas about alienation, globalisation and capitalism to a generation that had supposedly given up entirely on the political process.

Rock 'n' roll has always thrived on the unexpected, but there can be few more unlikely heroes than the five boys who have rewritten the rules about what popular music can be. From their early days at an exclusive school in Oxfordshire, rehearsing between lessons, via one-hit wonder status, through to releasing an album widely regarded as one of the greatest of all time, and then on to further work that pushes back the very boundaries of rock - this is Radiohead. Their genre-defying music, and Thom Yorke's desolate lyrics, have built up an intense, passionate following and brought massive commercial success. Musical messiahs or self-indulgent charlatans? Rock gods or posh boys slumming it? One of Radiohead's most maddening characteristics is that they never give straightforward answers.

Which is also, of course, what makes them so special. So fucking special...

CHAPTER 2

MORNING BELL

# MORNING BELL

*"I was a fine idea at the time,
Now I'm a brilliant mistake."*
*Elvis Costello*

Rock and roll's from the streets, innit? The blues of the dirt-poor Mississippi cotton-pickers, electrified in the slums of Chicago, then mashed up in the mean streets of New York, Liverpool and South Central LA.

Bollocks. The Beach Boys, The Beastie Boys, Pink Floyd, Blur, Limp Bizkit, The Clash... they might not all have been rich, but none of them knew where the ghetto was, either. John Lennon sang about being a working-class hero, but he grew up in lower-middle-class, suburban respectability. And as for the street-smart heroes of rap - Puff Daddy went to a private school and Tupac Shakur took ballet lessons. Hardly street tough - more avenue savvy.

But even if being born in the gutter isn't a prerequisite for credibility, most historians of popular music tend to bypass Abingdon School in Oxfordshire when they're researching the history of rock music. It's a fee-paying institution, founded some time in the 13th century. And in the early 1980s a small boy called Thomas Edward Yorke was deposited into these unlikely surroundings.

Thom was born on October 7, 1968 in Wellingborough, Northamptonshire. His upbringing was fairly comfortable in material terms, but he was afflicted by a partially-closed left eye, a problem that necessitated half a dozen operations during his childhood. His unusual appearance provoked some vicious playground taunts and, coupled with his small stature (he's never grown above five and a half feet), this led to him developing into a somewhat insecure adolescent. Spending his most difficult years in the conservative, conformist environment of an English independent school can't have helped.

"It was purgatory," he later told Paul Lester of *Melody Maker*. "It nurtured all the worst aspects of the British middle class: snobbery, lack of tolerance and right-wing stupidity." But he had an escape route in place, one that had been marked out when his mother bought him a Spanish guitar for his eighth birthday. Possibly encouraged by the punk revolution that was rumbling into life at the time, Thom had formed his own band by the time he was 11 years old. They were called Mushroom Cloud and comprised Thom on guitar and a friend who blew up old television sets to see what noises they would make. Rock 'n' roll had another disciple.

His first group at Abingdon was a punk outfit called TNT, but the only thing that exploded was Thom's patience at their lack of ambition. Instead he began swapping musical ideas with a tall, thin guitarist called Ed O'Brien and an Oscar Wilde lookalike named Colin Greenwood, who dabbled on the bass. Pretty quickly this formed the nucleus for On A Friday, so called because the strict timetable at Abingdon would only allow them one rehearsal session a week.

Other performers began to join the trio, including a pair of female saxophonists, a drummer named Phil Selway, and

Colin's kid brother Jonathan, who was allowed to contribute some harmonica honking. At this stage Thom's main influence was the acerbic singer-songwriter Elvis Costello, especially his *King Of America* album from 1986.

This wasn't just a meeting of musical minds; all five needed some sort of outlet to escape from the oppressive conformism of Abingdon. The most notable exponent of this was Colin, who would turn up at parties in a black bodystocking and snog boys, behaviour guaranteed to fry the mind of the school's rugby-playing hierarchy.

But, bad dress sense and bisexual horseplay aside, it was the music that really mattered. Although the talent scouts weren't exactly swarming around them, it was clear this wasn't just another lunchtime band whose career high spot would be the school Christmas concert. They landed fairly prestigious gigs at Oxford venues such as the Jericho Tavern, and were starting to build up a local following.

However, parental pressure came into effect when they left school, and the core members of the band all went away to college. Phil went to Liverpool Polytechnic (now John Moores University); Ed studied Economics at Manchester, then gearing itself up for the musical revolution that would be known as 'baggy'; Colin departed for the rarefied atmosphere of Peterhouse, at Cambridge, where he became entertainments secretary, booking On A Friday whenever possible, and, on one occasion, the legendary jazz trumpeter Humphrey Lyttleton; and Thom, displaying another outlet for his creative urges, went off to study Art at Exeter. Jonny, who was a couple of years younger, was still at Abingdon. Although the weekly rehearsals were no more, it was everybody's intention that On A Friday was just in a state of suspended animation, not dead.

Exeter College, Oxford
In 1988, On A Friday supported the Icicle Works during a gig at this Oxford college.

Clifton Hampden Village Hall
This building was where
On A Friday used to rehearse.

Abingdon School, Park Road, Abingdon
All five members of Radiohead attended
this prestigious independent school.

# CHAPTER 3

ANYONE CAN PLAY GUITAR

# ANYONE CAN PLAY GUITAR

*"You're so pretty when you're unfaithful to me."*
*The Pixies*

Exeter is probably not the most likely choice for a wannabe rock 'n' roll star to spend three of his formative years. It's a pleasant cathedral city in South Devon, surrounded by glorious moorland and famous for its cream teas. The closest it had come to being a rock mecca was in the late 1960s when a group of drama students called Principal Edward's Magic Theatre caused a stir in hippy circles with their Eastern-influenced folk-psychedelia. The city was also home to poet/ performer/ fanzine editor Jon Beast, who later attained nationwide notoriety as an auxiliary member of Carter The Unstoppable Sex Machine. But that was about it, music lovers. The local authorities seemed happy to maintain the area's status as a rock 'n' roll backwater, insisting that all clubs and venues close by one o'clock, supposedly to prevent three-cornered fights between locals, students and Marines from the nearby base at Lympstone.

But there was the occasional flicker of activity when Thom arrived. Student-run clubs like Shakedown and Creation provided an alternative to the Top 40 drivel on offer on the dancing-round-your-handbag circuit. There was also a small but fervent punk/ skate/goth scene, with its own cottage industry of bands and fanzines.

It wasn't the happiest of environments for someone escaping the claustrophobic conformism of an English public school and the class-based tensions of Oxford. Thom's drug of choice at the time was alcohol and this, coupled with his insistence on dressing like an old man (second-hand suits, trilby, big overcoat) occasionally got him into scrapes. He later expressed his opinion of his fellow students to *Q* magazine: "I was embarrassed to be a student because of what the little fuckers got up to. Walking down the street to be confronted by puke and shopping trolleys and police bollards. Fucking hell, I used to think, no wonder they hate us."

And the dislike doesn't seem to have been a one-way thing. An entry on the website Friends Reunited probably sums up the general reaction to him within the University:

"Thom Yorke was in Hope Hall in his first year (1988-89) at Exeter. He always struck me as a flawed genius - a man of great talent who was, however, all too often possessed of a repellent character. We all knew that he was going to be big, but no one guessed how big…"

"He would play his guitar in Hope Hall bar (the Badger) and sing various songs ('Happy Song' and 'Hope Hall' stick in my memory). I was Social Secretary on the Hall Committee and I booked his campus band for a Hope Hall formal disco. As other contributors have noted, he was DJ at the Lemmy on Fridays."

"It would be nice to say that he was a great guy and that everyone was happy for him when he made it big but that wouldn't be the truth. He was not universally liked but I am glad to say that the majority of people in hall appreciated his undoubted musical ability."

"I know a couple of good stories about him but, seeing as how he has access to the finest libel lawyers in the land, I daren't commit any to print!"

But not everybody held him at arm's length and he soon fell in with a like-minded bunch of musicians, becoming guitarist and occasional singer with a band called Headless Chickens. They were different from their musical contemporaries in the use of violinists (John Matthias and Laura Forrest-Hay) as part of the line-up, but the dominating influence was the wild-haired bassist Shack, known to his mum as Simon Shackleton. Shack was something of a polymath, also editing the university magazine, taking a show to the Edinburgh Festival and maintaining a key role in a shadowy political entity called the Exeter Mad Bastard Revolutionary Vanguard. Shack and Thom also DJ'ed at a club night called Fish Tank, where floorfillers included 'Bone Machine' by The Pixies and Mudhoney's 'Touch Me I'm Sick'.

The Headless Chickens became a popular draw on the local circuit, with a repertoire that mixed bizarre covers (Prince's 'Raspberry Beret'; the Everly Brothers' 'All I Have To Do Is Dream') with originals (such as an early version of 'High And Dry'). In 1989 they recorded their tongue-in-cheek anti-hippy anthem 'I Don't Want To Go To Woodstock' on an EP for the local Hometown Atrocities label, with fellow Exeter combos Beaver Patrol, Jackson Penis and Mad At The Sun also contributing songs. Expect to make over £100 if you've got one of these in your collection.

Shortly afterwards, Shack and Thom discovered a New Zealand band with the same name, so their act became known simply as Headless. But time was running out; Thom was about to graduate, and it was clear that his first loyalty was to his bandmates from Abingdon. In any case, On A Friday had been regrouping in Oxford during the holidays, and there was little doubt where his priorities lay. Shack formed a twisted techno outfit called Flickernoise, to which Thom briefly contributed some guitar noise, but it was clear their paths were to lie in different directions. Thom dabbled in dance sounds for a while, however, DJ'ing with an Exeter student called Felix Buxton, later to become half of Basement Jaxx.

Flickernoise mutated into Lunatic Calm, best known for the track 'Leave You All Behind' on the soundtrack of the Keanu Reeves movie *The Matrix*. Laura had a varied career, including a spell with the Irish band Big Geraniums and a period as assistant to the controversial magician/comedian Gerry Sadowitz. John Matthias, meanwhile, was to maintain his links with Thom, and carve out an interesting solo career while managing to earn a PhD in theoretical physics.

Thom hadn't paid much attention to his art studies while he was at Exeter, but in his final year he realised he ought to pull his finger out. The college had taken delivery of a new Apple Mac, and he scanned in a Michelangelo painting, then fucked around with the colouring, to create a psychedelic, Andy Warhol-style reworking. In the programme for the final year show, each student was allocated a page upon which they could describe their experiences, thoughts and ambitions. Under 'future plans', Thom wrote the straightforward desire:

'TO BE A POP STAR'.

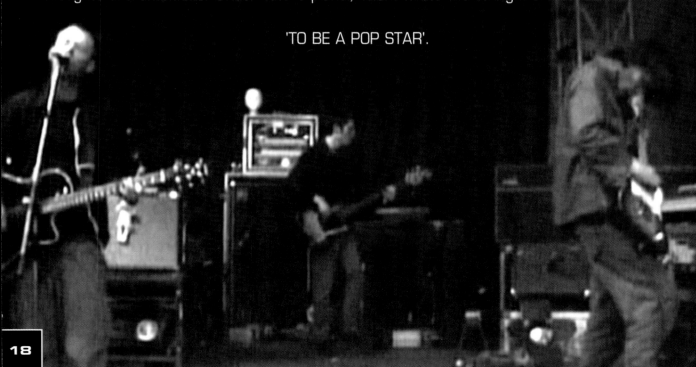

Ridgefield Road, Oxford
The band lived in this popular student area in the early 1990's.

Cult Clothing, Friars Entry, Oxford
Thom used to work at this street clothing shop prior to signing with EMI.

Browns Restaurant, Woodstock Road, Oxford
Ed used to wait on tables at this popular local restaurant.

Jericho Tavern, Walton Street, Oxford
On A Friday used to play regularly at this
popular live music venue.

PMT, Cowley Road, Oxford
This music shop is patronised by
Radiohead on a regular basis.

Apollo Theatre, George Street, Oxford
This 1800 seat venue was the location for a live
press preview show of The Bends in February 1995.

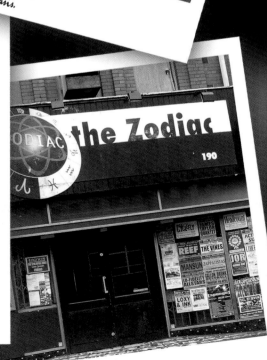

The Zodiac, Cowley Road, Oxford
This 500 seat venue was the location
for the Creep video.

# CHAPTER 4

LUCKY

# LUCKY

*"Your lyrics are crap. They're too honest, too personal, too direct and there's nothing left to the imagination."*
*Anonymous response to an On A Friday demo*

Thom, Ed, Colin and Phil had done their academic duties and achieved respectable enough results. But any parental hopes that they were about to become lawyers or accountants were shot down when On A Friday reconvened. Jonny, meanwhile, who had continued to serve his time in the restrictive environment of Abingdon School as his bandmates were being dissolute students, now took his turn at higher education. So as not to put the band through another three-year hiatus he stayed in Oxford, enrolling at the local Brookes University. And, unlike the others, he studied music (with a bit of philosophy to boot!) Like an indie variant on the Monkees, the five (the saxophone sisters had been declared surplus to requirements) all moved into the same house and threw themselves into the Oxford music scene with a wild-eyed vengeance.

At this point in the early 90s, Oxford wasn't such a bad place to be for an ambitious band. The Madchester sound had pretty much baggied itself out, and what would become Britpop was still a few years off. The music press, always desperate for an identifiable musical movement, had come up with 'shoegazing', a strand of indie rock that took the dense guitar textures of My Bloody Valentine to the next level. Many of the prime movers of this sound, like Ride and Slowdive, came from Oxford and the surrounding Thames Valley area. The shoegazing label came about because of the supposed tendency of the musicians to slouch and study their feet rather than interact with the audience.

Many observers sneered that this was just a return to the up-its-own-arse self-indulgence of 70s progressive rock, which had been a critical no-go area since the punk explosion in 1977. But the shoegazers managed to shift a respectable number of units, mainly to shy, middle-class students who'd never really got to grips with the aggression of hip-hop or the huggy mateyness of acid house. One successful product of the scene was Slowdive's *Just For A Day* album, which had been produced by Chris Hufford. Hufford, who worked with his partner Bryce Edge in Courtyard Studios near the boys' old school at Abingdon, became aware of On A Friday through their first demo tape. It was a fairly primitive effort, although it contained an early version of 'Stop Whispering', which would later appear on their debut album and get a single release in the US. The tape had also earned the band their first published review, in the Oxford fanzine *Nightshift*. The anonymous critic identified "an unusually talented lead singer" and a strain of "good commercial indie guitar music" (this was way before Oasis and Blur were scrapping at the top of the charts, remember).

Even at this stage, On A Friday were a different kettle of plectrums from their contemporaries, steering clear of the self-indulgence offered by the likes of Slowdive and taking their influences from acts like The Pixies, the legendary Boston quintet widely credited with creating the musical groundwork of grunge.

Hufford spotted some promise in the demo, but he wasn't beating a path to the door of their decrepit semi-detached hovel. However, in August 1991 he noticed that they were playing at the Jericho, and decided to see if they could cut it in a live environment. Stunned by the passion and quality on show, he offered them professional help with their recording work, the result of which was a five-track demo with the unlikely title *Manic Hedgehog*.

To keep themselves supplied with fags and guitar strings, the band members were all holding down mundane jobs. Colin, for example, had an existence behind the counter in the Our Price record shop, selling Bryan Adams and Color Me Badd to the fine, cloth-eared citizens of Oxford and coming into regular contact with sales representatives from record companies. So when a rep from the mighty EMI corporation popped in one day, it didn't seem unusual. However, Keith Wozencroft wasn't trying to offload the new Cliff Richard single - he was dropping by to say goodbye, as he'd been promoted to the company's A&R (artists and repertoire) division in London. Green as he was in the ways of the biz, Colin knew this meant that Keith now had the power to sign bands, and he immediately handed him a copy of the *Manic Hedghog* tape.

Suddenly, things started to happen.

# CHAPTER 5

## DOLLARS AND CENTS

# DOLLARS AND CENTS

*"Mummy, Daddy come and look at me now."*
*Talking Heads*

A&R people tend to have an edgy pack mentality, following each others' leads but always aware that they're all in competition. None of them wants to be in the position of Dick Rowe, the man who notoriously turned down The Beatles; but similarly, they don't want to be responsible for an over-hyped, expensive embarrassment. Word of this complex, serious five-piece from a posh school immediately started circulating around the EMI offices and the company's competitors soon picked up the scent. By the time On A Friday next played the Jericho Tavern, in November, the story went around that there were more A&R people in the audience than paying punters. Despite the crazy offers that were being thrown around, the band stuck with the original interest shown by EMI, and signed a deal with the company to release product under the legendary Parlophone imprint, home, of course, of The Beatles. Chris Hufford and Bryce Edge were to be their managers.

The A&R storm had been picked up by the London music press, including the venerable weekly *Melody Maker* (now deceased), which sent John Harris to cover a gig at another Oxford venue, called, with staggering facetiousness, The Venue. He loved their performance but couldn't bear the name, an opinion that seemed to be pretty widespread in the business. The band members were determined not to compromise their musical ideals to get ahead in the industry, but the name of the group was pretty insignificant, all things considered, and it was only down to sentimental attachment that they were still called On A Friday.

They kicked around a few new ideas. Jude, named after the Thomas Hardy novel *Jude The Obscure*, was considered and rejected (it had already been used in the early 70s, for a power trio formed by guitarist Robin Trower when he left the psychedelic legends Procul Harum). The name 'Music' was championed by Thom, but vetoed by his bandmates. (They had no idea that a Leeds quartet called The Music would be described by the *NME* as "the most exciting British guitar band" nearly a decade later.) Finally, trawling through their massive combined record collection, they seized upon True Stories, a mid-80s album by the American art-rock band Talking Heads. One of the tracks on it was 'Radio Head', a tuneful piece of whimsy that had reached the dizzying heights of number 52 on the UK charts in 1987. By now desperate, the band squeezed the title into one word and decided to go with it. Whatever happened, it was better than On A Friday.

So it was as Radiohead that the band released their first product for EMI, in May 1992. The *Drill* EP provoked a few positive reviews, and the track 'Prove Yourself' was played a couple of times on daytime Radio One, but marketing and distribution problems caused the record to stall just outside the Top 100. Nobody in the band had imagined things were going to be easy, but this was a sharp reminder that even the economic might of the EMI empire couldn't guarantee success.

Radiohead were by now supporting shoegazing pioneers Catherine Wheel on a UK tour and had been hoping that a moderate success for *Drill* would mean the audience actually knew some of their songs (an unusual scenario for a support act).

However, the EP's relative failure did have a positive side, although nobody realised it at the time. Because they didn't feel their live playlist had to adhere to the tracks on their record (since nobody had heard it anyway) the band felt free to try out some new material. One that seemed to provoke a flicker of interest from the audience was a yearning slowie about a hopeless crush that had afflicted Thom in his Exeter years and when the band came to record their next single, it was this song that grabbed the attention of the producers, Paul Kolderie and Sean Slade. These two Americans were holding a fine track record with acts such as Dinosaur Jr, they had replaced Hufford and Edge behind the mixing deck, and they had a pretty good radar for alternative hit sounds. When they heard 'Creep' for the first time they were dumbfounded.

It's probably unnecessary to describe the song in great detail - even people who couldn't name another Radiohead track will know it, its classic status having almost taken it out of the orbit of its musical creators. It's been covered by such unlikely patrons as The Cure, The Pretenders, Tears For Fears, Irish comedian Patrick Kielty (complete with gospel choir) and ex-Take That heart-throb Mark Owen; but Radiohead's remains the definitive version, mainly because Jonny's discordant guitar abuse blows away any hints of self-indulgence that the sorrowful lyric might imply. Several years later, Thom told *Rolling Stone*: "If that guitar hadn't exploded where it exploded, there's no way it would have got on alternative radio. And we wouldn't be anywhere."

In fact, this six-string explosion was almost accidental; Jonny hated the song at first and his feedback was a half-hearted attempt to sabotage it. But he was won round, and Kolderie, Slade and the band decided that it should be the main track on the single, shunting 'Inside My Head' to also-ran status.

Unfortunately, despite the emotional wallop it packed for the band's producers, 'Creep' was by no means an immediate success. When it was released as a single in September 1992, mainstream radio in the UK was unconvinced by its merits and it peaked at number 78 - an improvement on the *Drill* EP but hardly a resounding vote of confidence from the record-buying public by any standards.

Things were looking bleak on the sales front, and the A&R scrum that had surrounded the band only a few months before was now looking like a pretty lame joke.

Nonetheless, the EMI suits were patient enough to let the band (with Kolderie and Slade) remain in the studio to put together an album, released in early 1993.

*Pablo Honey* kicks off with the song 'You', which pretty much defines Radiohead's unique qualities. There's a pretty, jangly intro, exploding into some neo-heavy-metal riffing, buoyed up by jazzy drums. Thom's lyrics ("You and me and everything, caught in the fire") hint at the bleak self-destruction in the Smiths' 'There Is A Light That Never Goes Out', but his larynx-shredding screams take the song into primal territories where Morrissey has never ventured. 'Creep', by now a high spot of the band's live show, and not yet the MTV-approved millstone it would become, comes next, but after this double-whammy, the quality and originality on offer starts to tail off.

'How Do You', a vicious attack on an anonymous "bigot", has glam-rock guitars and sneering vocals that sound not a little like Radiohead's contemporaries Suede, another British guitar band that would make an impact across the Atlantic. There's a Velvet Underground-style instrumental breakdown at the end, but it doesn't redeem this forgettable track. Sharp-eared listeners might be able to pick up a sample of the New York telephone pranksters the Jerky Boys, whose routines gave the album its title.

Even more disappointing is 'Stop Whispering', a mid-tempo number that bears all the hallmarks of U2. Like much of the Irish band's material, it's an arena-style, lighters-aloft moment, that works in the context of a gig (it's still a live favourite) but sounds pretty flat in the studio. There's some more Velvety axe abuse to perk things up at the end, but it's too little, too late.

Folky acoustic riffing heralds 'Thinking About You', another slab of Thom's patented self-abasement in the face of an unattainable love object. It's an intense, affecting performance, but the song itself doesn't really go anywhere. Better things are promised by the sedately funky bass of 'Anyone Can Play Guitar'. Its apocalyptic lyrics ("And if London burns I'll be standing on the beach with my guitar") appeal to the bleak misanthrope in all of us and the three-note riff implant itself on the listener's brain. This track became the second single release from the album, in early 1993, and it reached number 32 - an improvement, but still hardly the kind of result the band or their record company might have hoped for.

'Ripcord's quiet-loud opening owes much to The Pixies. Unlike most of the lyrics on the album, which deal with personal alienation and depression, the line "politics and power that you don't understand" foreshadows Thom's growing interest in the impact of global political and economic forces and the way they invisibly control whole populations. This theme would become much more explicit in Thom's later lyrics and in interviews.

'Vegetable' and 'Prove Yourself' go back to the interior monologues of the quintessentially alienated indie kid: The "I'm better off dead" refrain on the latter is almost a self-parody of the tortured Morrissey fan. The pseudo-Eastern intro to 'I Can't' raises the interest levels a little, but lyrics like "If you give up on me now I'll be gutted like I've never been before" is almost edging into Adrian Mole territory.

'Lurgee' comes as something of a relief: we're back to the neo-U2 rousing sound of 'Stop Whispering', but the lyrics have almost positive overtones: "I feel better," chokes Thom, and the world wonders whether it will last. 'Blow Out' also goes some way to redeeming the maudlin feel of the second half of the album; from a catchy bossa nova intro to an explosion of searing guitar histrionics (Jonny uses a coin as a plectrum, a trick borrowed from Brian May of Queen) the band members prove that their instrumental prowess can triumph over less-than-brilliant material. "Everything I touch turns to stone," sings Thom, which is somewhat ironic, as the band seems able to turn unpromising songs into something rather more precious.

Critical reaction was positive but not wildly enthusiastic. Jonny's imaginitive guitar work was praised, but the songs themselves were felt to be inconsistent. It's a verdict even the most devoted fan would probably share. There's plenty of talent and promise at work here, but only two or three really outstanding songs.

The gaps are patched up by some impressive fretboard fireworks, but at the time there were any number of bands trying to replicate the Wall Of Guitars patented by My Bloody Valentine. As Mat Snow put it in *Q*, "Theirs is a self-preoccupied sound, morosely resentful of romantic failure and finding solace only in giving the axe a spanking."

The album went into the UK charts at number 25 - still not storming the pop barricades, but perfectly respectable for a band without a big hit single to its name. Radiohead might have settled down to being a decent, middle-ranking rock band, not regular visitors to *Top Of The Pops* but staying in the black through album and ticket sales to a loyal hardcore following. But something odd was happening several thousand miles away.

The world of music radio in North America is much more fragmented than in the UK; it's a mosaic of local stations, many of them with very specific formats and target markets; in any decent-sized city you'll find stations that specialize in pop, rock or country, stations that target black or Latino listeners and, usually, one or two playing sounds classified as 'alternative' or 'college rock'. In San Francisco, the most influential alternative station was 106.9 KROQ, and its ability to tap into the popular tastes of the grunge generation meant that programmers across the continent studied its playlists intently. So when KROQ DJs began playing a slow track by an unknown English band in the spring of 1993, people took notice.

Actually, it wasn't the version of 'Creep' from *Pablo Honey* that was played in the US - the "so fucking special" line was deemed to be too startling for the good people of San Francisco - so Capitol, EMI's North American counterpart, released a new cut with the offending adverb replaced by 'very'. Swearwords aside, it was a track that tapped a mood with an audience besotted by the self-loathing of acts like Nirvana and the quirky introspection of REM. Suddenly, the band was in serious demand on the other side of the Atlantic.

In their home country they were still supporting flavour-of-the-month acts like Kingmaker. In the States they were suddenly a fixture on top-rating TV shows and, of all things, on MTV. They were even persuaded to play the song at an MTV Beach Party, a scenario later described ruefully in *Spin* magazine by Jonny Greenwood: "At least we played well. But I don't think the irony was lost on people. All these gorgeous, bikini-ed girls shaking their mammary glands, and we're playing 'Creep' and looking terrible."

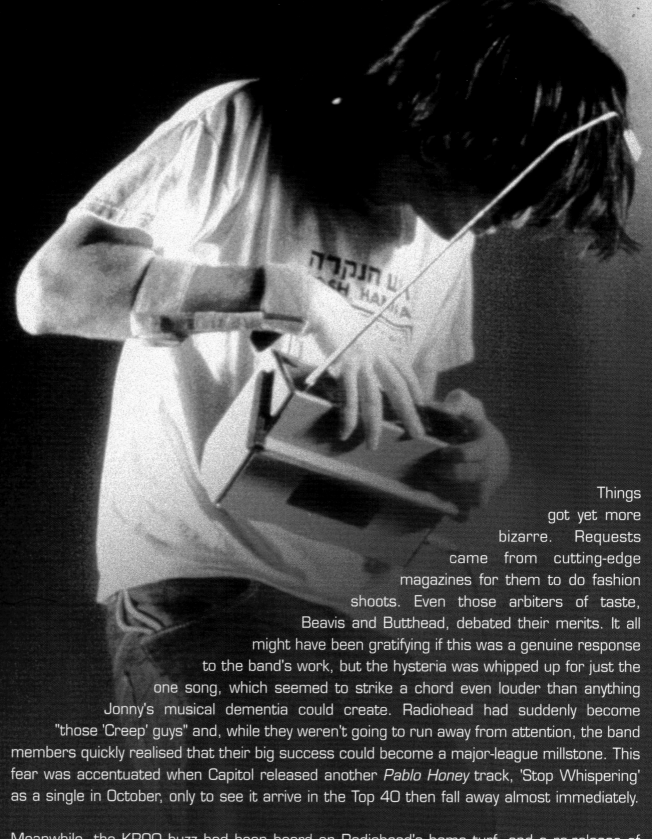

Things got yet more bizarre. Requests came from cutting-edge magazines for them to do fashion shoots. Even those arbiters of taste, Beavis and Butthead, debated their merits. It all might have been gratifying if this was a genuine response to the band's work, but the hysteria was whipped up for just the one song, which seemed to strike a chord even louder than anything Jonny's musical dementia could create. Radiohead had suddenly become "those 'Creep' guys" and, while they weren't going to run away from attention, the band members quickly realised that their big success could become a major-league millstone. This fear was accentuated when Capitol released another *Pablo Honey* track, 'Stop Whispering' as a single in October, only to see it arrive in the Top 40 then fall away almost immediately.

Meanwhile, the KROQ buzz had been heard on Radiohead's home turf, and a re-release of 'Creep' reached number 7 on the UK charts in the autumn of 1993. Finally, people knew who they were; there were appearances on *Top Of The Pops*, features in the music press, chances for Thom to vent his spleen on those who'd shat on him in the past. But one hit single doesn't make a successful career, and Radiohead still had work to do.

# CHAPTER 6

## PROVE YOURSELF

# PROVE YOURSELF

*"It's just that look on people's faces when they're trying to sell you something. It's a look of more or less complete madness. It's funny but really sad at the same time."*
Thom Yorke

So what does a band with a successful single, a moderately achieving album and a record company slightly nervous at their chances of recouping a healthy investment do next? Time to hit the road, guys. The band's campaign to raise their profile on the live circuit got off to a bad start in August; a prestigious slot at the Reading Festival had to be cancelled when Thom lost his voice. The following month, however, they began a major North American jaunt with the then-successful indie quartet Belly, fronted by ex-Throwing Muses icon Tanya Donnelly. The band members found touring an odd experience - on the whole the actual performances were OK, but phenomena like groupies really didn't appeal to them. It was possibly helpful that the headlining act was 50% female - Radiohead have always avoided the raucous, laddish antics that characterise some other bands' on-the-road behaviour.

'Creep' fever was still in the air: although it never got higher than 32 on the *Billboard* chart, in October they were presented with a prestigious gold disc and the single went on to shift 2 million units worldwide. But there remained a nagging doubt about their ability to keep up the momentum. The album wasn't an unqualified success and their first post-*Pablo Honey* release, the single *Pop Is Dead*, suffered pretty damning reviews and failed to make the Top 40 in the UK. To be fair, though, "radio has salmonella" isn't the sort of line that gets you priority plays on drivetime. And as for "one final line of coke to jerk him off..." It's almost as if the band didn't want to play by the rules any more.

After finishing the tour with Belly, Radiohead returned to Oxfordshire, taking over an old fruit farm and converting it into a studio facility. For the follow-up to *Pablo Honey*, they'd decided to work with John Leckie, a studio veteran whose career began in the early 70s, working at EMI's legendary Abbey Road studios on albums by ex-members of The Beatles and Pink Floyd's groundbreaking albums *Dark Side Of The Moon* and *Wish You Were Here*. This association with the prog rock dinosaurs of the Floyd could have damaged his reputation in the post-punk era, but he went on to produce seminal albums by XTC, Magazine and The Fall. More recently he had worked on the Stone Roses' era-defining debut LP, and also with Radiohead's immediate predecessors as figureheads of the Oxford scene, Ride.

Although Radiohead were firmly labelled as representatives of the indie/alternative scene that was spawned by punk, it was as much Leckie's earlier work that attracted them to him. Pink Floyd might have been lacking in street credibility by the mid-90s, but Thom found lots to identify with in their sprawling albums. Like Radiohead, the band members were all middle-class, from an ancient university city (in Floyd's case Cambridge) and, especially when Roger Waters was the dominating influence, obsessed by themes of personal alienation and political control. Moreover, their albums in the 70s were landmarks in the way they took studio technology to new levels, giving the basic guitar-bass-drums rock group an orchestral potential. *Pablo Honey* had its positive aspects, but in essence it was just another indie rock album. Now the band wanted to do something a little different. Ignoring the Oxfordshire facilities for the moment, they based themselves in the Abbey Road studios where Leckie had originally learned his craft, and began work.

or a start, they'd give their next album the time and care it deserved - this contrasts with *Pablo Honey*, which was knocked out in under a month. Rather than concentrating on refining well-executed versions of songs they'd already played on stage, the band began experimenting with computers, tape effects, samples and drum loops. They brought in outside musicians for the first time, including John Matthias, Thom's former colleague from the Headless Chickens. Also in the studio was an engineer named Nigel Godrich, whose technical skills would become increasingly important to the band. All the time, the band maintained an iron resolve that they wouldn't be hurried, despite panicky noises coming from the higher echelons of EMI.

In May 1994 they were due to begin a major tour, although still lacking  much recorded material with which they were entirely happy. There were unfortunate precedents here - Leckie had originally worked on the Stone Roses' second album, a project that had become a byword for procrastination and self-indulgence. Its eventual release, at the end of 1994, would be accompanied by critical derision, disappointing sales, and the eventual collapse of the band.

But Radiohead weren't going to be dissuaded by the excesses of other bands. Their itinerary kicked off at London's Astoria Theatre (a gig captured on video) and then took them to Japan, Australia and New Zealand, before returning to Britain for high-profile appearances at Glastonbury and Reading (for which Thom's throat held out this time). With their live commitments honoured, they returned to recording, this time setting up shop in their new Oxfordshire base. Their live work had given them a new burst of adrenalin and inspiration, and they soon had tracks ready for mixing, bringing in their previous production team of Kolderie and Slade to give the songs the dash of sonic punchiness that would appeal to US alternative radio stations.

But if EMI thought that the band's next offering would be an airwave-friendly unit-shifter along the lines of 'Creep', they were sorely disappointed. 'My Iron Lung', released as a single in September 1994, could be classified as the anti-'Creep', a dig at the fair-weather, MTV-fixated fans who could only see them as a one-song band. "This is our new song, just like the old one," sneers Thom; the trebly intro and brief guitar duel could indeed have made it onto *Pablo Honey*. But the musical landscape was changing. Nirvana's charismatic frontman Kurt Cobain had committed suicide in April, bringing the self-loathing edifice of grunge to a halt. Another spokesman for the disaffected, Richey Edwards of the Manic Street Preachers, was becoming a cause for concern with episodes of self-harm and heavy drinking, and would disappear in February of the following year.

The word on the industry's lips was 'Britpop', a strain of indie rock where self-examination was replaced by droll celebration, and intense, Floydy space jams were jettisoned in favour of crisp, mid-60s influenced riffs. A quintet of Mancunian bruisers called Oasis were storming venues, with Blur and Pulp not far behind. There was even a Britpop menace closer to home, as Chris Hufford had taken on another Oxford band, Supergrass - their party anthem, 'Alright', released the following year, would become a defining moment of 90s pop.

Sensing the changing mood, Radio One declined to playlist 'My Iron Lung' and the single failed to make the British Top 20. For a band that hadn't released anything in a year, this was a worry - they'd complained about people only wanting them for 'Creep', but now it looked as if nobody wanted them at all. It wasn't a happy band that embarked on a UK tour in October, with a brief interlude in Mexico, and some acoustic gigs in New York. It now seemed as if the forthcoming album could make or break the band - with the latter looking the most likely.

Ironically, the last song to make it to the final track listing was the oldest. Thom had originally played 'High And Dry' with the Headless Chickens at Exeter and its inclusion seemed to indicate a sense of continuity with the past - Radiohead weren't about to jump on the Britpop bandwagon, and *The Bends* would be a natural progression from *Pablo Honey*, not a radical leap. This caused some problems for Capitol, the band's record company in North America, who almost refused to release the album, since it was lacking any obvious hit singles. In the end, they caved in, and *The Bends* hit American shops in April 1995, three weeks after its European and Japanese releases.

*The Bends* opens with the big, punchy chords of 'Planet Telex', but, smashing expectations as ever, the voice that joins them is compressed, almost alien. The best comparison is with that earlier parable of alienation, David Bowie's 'Space Oddity', although Radiohead's lyrics are even bleaker. "Everything is broken, everyone is broken," croaks Thom, notching up the intensity of apocalyptic imagery we saw in 'Anyone Can Play Guitar'. Incidentally, this track was originally called 'Planet Xerox', but the title was changed at the last minute so as not to breach copyright. It wouldn't be the last time Radiohead was forced to confront the might of global capitalism.

There's more alienation on the title track. 'The bends' is excess nitrogen in the bloodstream, a condition that affects sea divers when they undergo decompression too quickly, usually when surfacing, and the song 'The Bends' uses this as an analogy for Radiohead's (too?-) rapid rise to international fame. "I want to be part of the human race," pleads Thom, but he's now labelled "that 'Creep' guy" and there's jack shit he can do about it.

Again his voice is compressed almost beyond recognition, adding a level of irony to his pleas for humanity.

The irony carries on in 'High And Dry', a deceptively pretty acoustic-led ditty, and the first time we hear Thom's almost-natural voice. "All your insides fall to pieces," he coos, and it could refer to the song itself. Superficially it's a standard, functional pop tune, but the content gnaws away from the inside. Self-reflexivity, they call it in English class. Isn't it time some of Thom's lyrics made it onto the curriculum?

The gap between appearance and reality is investigated further on 'Fake Plastic Trees'. It's a lyric that seems to have its roots in a tired old joke, but ends as an existential lament. The plastic surgeon's inability to defeat gravity and time is a metaphor for our own inability to fight the powers of... Fate? Life? The System? But are we being told to accept the unreality? "She tastes like the real thing, my fake plastic love." A subtle dig at the Coca-Colonisation of the planet? Or a rueful reminder that love can make everything feel all right?

The pain imagery of 'High And Dry' comes back in spades on 'Bones'. In a possible reference to the London Astoria gig in May 1994, where Thom sustained a greenstick fracture of the ankle, it presents a classic dilemma: is it better to feel pain ("krippled kracked, shoulders, wrists, knees and back") or to feel nothing ("prozak painkillers"). As the 19th-century philosopher Nietzsche said, "life is a choice between boredom and pain," but Thom doesn't offer us an answer.

There's a potential respite from the agony on '(Nice Dream)', as a beautiful wash of John Matthias's violin and some soothing backing vocals create an idyllic image of sunshine, gardens and angels. But, as the title says, it's just a dream, and the brackets imply that it's not even a fully-accredited song, just a blissful interlude from the suffering. In any case, happiness doesn't suit Yorke that well. As Phil Selway remarked about his frontman to Rolling Stone's John Wiederhorn, after the album's release: "He doesn't like to feel satisfied. When things are going well, he will throw things off balance so that he'll be in a state of flux. That's the way he works best." Or, as Thom himself put it: "People sometimes ask me if I'm happy and I tell them to fuck off. If I was happy, I'd be in a fucking car advert."

And sure enough, we're back to the limits of physical pain with 'Just', which seems to address domestic violence, although by the time we get to the earbleeding guitar solo the song seems to encompass all varieties of human suffering, from nuclear war to a stubbed toe. "How to get to purest hell," indeed. The video for this track was enigmatic even by Radiohead's standards, depicting a man lying on a pavement and eventually persuading all the passers-by to join him. Opting out of the human race? A mass lie-down protest? You choose.

The relative commercial failure of 'My Iron Lung' probably hinted that the band's lyrical bleakness wasn't going to slot into the jovial post-Parklife zeitgeist, but the irony is that it addresses that superficially upbeat state of mind more acutely than any of the Britpop bands had done. "Suck, suck your teenage thumb" is surely a lament for the lost generation who seize upon the three-chord retro certainties of Oasis or the sparkly insignificance of manufactured pop, because it's easier than actually facing up to reality.

With 'Bullet Proof... I Wish I Was' we're back to the synthesis of soulful acoustic guitars and unbearable physical pain. Not only does Thom despise the fame machine ("Pay me money and take a shot"), it sounds as if life itself is making him feel like some kind of hospital patient ("Wax me, mould me, heat the pins.")

'Black Star' opens with an image that's arresting for its sheer banality. "I get home from work and you're still standing in your dressing gown" sounds like something from a minor-league sitcom, but it does remind the listeners of a few home truths. For one thing, the members of Radiohead are as much wage slaves and workers as the burger flippers and telesales executives who buy their products. And, for all Thom's protestations of isolation and loathing, he's been in a stable (albeit deeply private) relationship with his partner Rachel since his time at college. So, is he just trying to get inside the head of some suburban commuter? Is he playing a role? And, if so, should we be careful about taking some of his other lyrics at face value? The theme of bourgeois banality persists in 'Sulk' - "Just like your Dad, you'll never change." But, as ever, there's a bleaker subtext. The song was inspired by the Hungerford massacre of 1987, when a lonely young man called Michael Ryan shot 13 people in his nondescript home town in South East England. Horror can co-exist with mundane, everyday existence - but is horror a valid release from everyday existence?

The churning final chords of 'Sulk' die away, to be replaced by Ed's urgent guitar intro to 'Street Spirit (Fade Out)'. Thom summons up his last reserves of hope, urging children to save the planet that their elders have come so close to destroying. It's a grudging rallying call, topping off an album almost unequalled in its nightmarish pessimism. In Thom's words: "It's a reflection of us. It's cynical and nervous and it doesn't make sense. And you get the feeling at the end of it that something's wrong, but you can't quite work out what it is."

*Rolling Stone* offered guarded praise, hymning the guitar sounds as "twitches of fuzzy tremolo and eruptions of amplified paranoia". However, critic Ted Drozdowski wasn't as happy with what he described as Thom's "oblique lyrics" and "honeyed melodies", judging that the lack of open-heated emotion would hamper Radiohead's chances of developing a post-'Creep' identity in North America. Back in Britain, however, reaction was more positive. *Q* magazine dubbed it "a powerful, bruised, majestically desperate record of frighteningly good songs". In the *NME*, Mark Sutherland was even more ecstatic, peppering his review with adjectives like "epic" and "classic" and declaring that "Thom Yorke's ghostly falsetto attains heights of emotion practically unheard of in this irony-infested age". Jonny Greenwood's contribution also came in for high praise: he "frequently turns the very concept of The Great Guitar Riff upside down and inside out."

The album's performance reflected this critical disparity; in the UK it reached number 4, but it struggled on the *Billboard* chart. In fact, the USA was the only territory where *The Bends* failed to match the sales of *Pablo Honey*.

A little later, Colin Greenwood summed up the band's feelings about the album: "*The Bends* was many things, but it wasn't really chirpy, was it? It was more like a darkness lumbering over the horizon with gun turrets strafing the Britpop hordes with misery. Er, sorry. Got a bit carried away there..."

Dry English drollery aside, part of the problem was that Thom's lyrical concerns were seen to be outdated, even dangerous. He'd originally intended 'Sulk' to end with the line 'Just shoot your gun' but removed the words so as not to make a link with the death of Kurt Cobain. And the pathological references to physical suffering in 'Bones' might have been seen in a new light when compared with the Manic Street Preachers' 1994 album *The Holy Bible*, which dealt with anorexia, the Holocaust, abortion and serial killers. In retrospect, the Manics' work was seen as a clear warning that lyricist Richey Edwards was in serious trouble, and his subsequent disappearance was taken to be a dire warning about the effect 'the Cult of Miserablism' could have on impressionable young people. Surely it was better to have them whistling jaunty singalongs about Girls and Boys and Shakermakers? This was the age of 'the New Bloke', of Chris Evans and all he stood for, and Radiohead weren't invited to the party.

Even the look of the album seemed out of kilter. This was the band's first major collaboration with Stanley Donwood, whose nightmarish, cartoony images have become as much part of the band's identity as Thom's lyrics. While other bands were employing kitsch, quintessentially English images like greyhounds and 1970 footballers, Radiohead decorated their product with medical photographs and line drawings that looked more like the result of an art therapy class in a psychiatric hospital.

The big priority had to be the next album. *The Bends* had been far from a disaster of course. In terms of sales and credibility, the band had saved their bacon, levering themselves away from the dreaded 'one-hit wonder' tag. Capitol and Parlophone were disappointed at the lack of another classic single, but this absence was presumably something of a relief to the band members themselves. The album's lack of impact in the States was disappointing, but not fatal. However, if Radiohead were really going to make a mark amidst the 'ironic' Union Jacks of Britpop, they were going to have to come up with something even more special.

So they did.

Big time.

# CHAPTER 7

# BLACK STAR

# BLACK STAR

*"I'm fifty thousand times more intelligent than you and even I don't know the answer."*
*Douglas Adams*
*"And I think my spaceship knows which way to go."*
*David Bowie*

Although they were pretty contemptuous of Britpop, in some ways Radiohead benefited from it. For a start, it meant that British guitar bands were commercially viable again, not just a niche market for NME-reading students. They were definitely getting known beyond the indie ghetto, although sometimes the message got a little twisted in translation. For example, amusing 80s throwback Jason Donovan tried to resuscitate a career that was receding faster than his hairline by announcing that he was well into "the Radioheads". Sadly, the band didn't reciprocate with a cover version of 'Too Many Broken Hearts', or even the theme from *Neighbours*.

The band's first priority was to try to rebuild their profile across the Atlantic. Thom had formed a kind of mutual appreciation society with Michael Stipe of REM. The Georgia-based art rockers had developed from cult heroes to stadium rock titans, mainly on the back of their early 90s albums *Out Of Time* and *Automatic For The People*. So, when Radiohead were invited to open for REM on their North American tour in September 1995, there was a clear message - play your cards right and you too can translate indie credibility into total domination. A November jaunt with Soul Asylum (more notorious for singer Dave Pirner's dalliance with Winona Ryder than for their contributions to the progress of popular music) was slightly less happy. Still, it kept up the English band's profile in the North American alt-rock constituency.

But chart positions and consumer demographics weren't the most important thing to Radiohead. Since the end of communist rule in the late 1980s and early 1990s, the area that was once called Yugoslavia had descended into a brutal and bloody civil war, largely along ethnic and religious lines. As with all wars, it wasn't just the fighters themselves who were suffering: tens of thousands of children were being killed, injured, orphaned or displaced. As with George Harrison's Concert For Bangladesh in 1971 and Bob Geldof's Band Aid projects in the mid-1980s, the music industry suddenly proved that it wasn't the moral cesspit one might have thought. On 4 September 1995, over 20 acts went into various recording studios to create something that might raise funds and awareness. Because of the tight scheduling (nobody was allowed more than 24 hours to record their efforts) the results were much rawer and less self-satisfied than many charity projects. The acts involved included guitar bands such as Oasis, Blur, Suede and the Manic Street Preachers, and dance acts like Massive Attack, Orbital and the Chemical Brothers. But many observers agreed that the most potent contribution to the album, entitled *Help!*, came from Radiohead. 'Lucky', guided into existence by Ed O'Brien's understated strumming (see, there's more than one guitar hero in this band!) has what might almost be described as a happy lyric, although these things are relative. "I feel my luck could change..." intones Thom, "It's gonna be a glorious day." Although only Radiohead could make a line like "pull me out of the aircrash" celebratory. Maybe if they were in a really bad mood they wouldn't get pulled out...

Once again, Radio One all but ignored 'Lucky', even when it was released as the lead track on an EP. Success of sorts came when the album was nominated for the prestigious Mercury Prize, indicating that it was musically worthwhile, as well as being morally sound. It didn't take the trophy, but Pulp, who had won with *Different Class*, generously donated their prize money to the War Child charity.

By then, however, Radiohead had other things to think about. With the exception of an unlikely tour in the company of Canadian angst-by-numbers songstress Alanis Morissette, the next 18 months would be taken up with recording a new album.

With Nigel Godrich, the engineer on *The Bends*, installed as producer, Radiohead based themselves in St Catherine's Court, a mansion owned by the actress Jane Seymour, a venue widely reported to be haunted. This probably helped with the paranoid bleakness of Thom's lyrics, but any thoughts that the historical, ghostly setting would spawn a backward-looking album were to be rudely dashed. This was to be a piece of work that looked forward to the oncoming millennium - hopelessly, with undisguised disgust, but still looking forward.

While they were between albums, Ed O'Brien had predicted: "I think the third album will be celebratory and maybe not so inward-looking, that would be great. I think thinking is a good thing, but there are times when you say 'fuck it'." If the lanky guitarist thought this meant their next opus would be a Britpoptastic laff riot, he was disappointed.

The title for a start. 'OK, Computer' is a quotation from *The Hitch-Hiker's Guide To The Galaxy*, originally a radio script, later a series of books, a TV show, a stage play, a (very early) computer game and, at some time in the near future, a movie. All sprang from the fertile mind of Douglas Adams, whose comic take on science fiction might seem at odds with Radiohead's gloomy perception of life. But Adams was never a complacent joker. He uses his fiction to poke fun at the idiocies of mankind; one of the key scenes in *The Hitch-Hiker's Guide* is the destruction of the Earth to make way for a bypass, but the implication is that every time mankind builds a bypass, there's an equivalent level of destruction. Adams later expanded his ideas on conservation in the book *Last Chance To See...*, almost a checklist of the species brought to the brink of extinction by the pigheaded selfishness of homo sapiens.

But this wasn't to be an air-punching eco-album, clearly elucidating all the wrongs in the world. Thom's most coherent explanation for the work was: "Background noise. Everything is background noise. Our whole lives, how our minds work. And the whole album is about that - levels of background chatter."

The opening track, 'Airbag', sets the scene: "In the next world war..." apocalypse, annihilation, desolation. But over cut-up, sampled drums, Thom announces that "I am back to save the universe". It's the Rock Star As Jesus equation, as used by the original Leper Messiah, David Bowie, in his 1972 album *The Rise And Fall Of Ziggy Stardust And The Spiders From Mars*. It's all ironic, of course - Thom was heartily sick of the worship that had followed him around since 'Creep', and this is the first of many masks that he adopts throughout the album. The problem, of course, is identifying which (if any) of them speaks with Thom's 'real' voice.

'Paranoid Android' is another Douglas Adams reference, to the much-loved character Marvin. He's another creation that could have been spawned in Bowie's science fiction period, enduring a million-year exile in a carpark at the end of the universe, and generally suffering the social and intellectual inadequacies of the flesh-and-blood characters he's doomed to serve. 'Paranoid Android' is actually a fusion of three songs, anchored by Colin's menacing bass riff. The range of the lyrics is extraordinary, encompassing jabs against royalty ("When I am King you will be first against the wall" were allegedly Prince William's words to a fellow-pupil on his first day at nursery school) and yuppies ("kicking squealing Gucci little piggy"). The latter line was later explained by Thom to *Q*'s Phil Sutcliffe as the result of observing a woman in a bar: "Someone spilt a drink over her and she turned into this fiend. I mean, everyone was out of their minds on coke and I'm sure it was that. But it seems to be happening to me a lot. Seeing a look in someone's eye and, fucking hell, what was that? Getting me right... like someone walking on your grave." The final sequence of the song owes a definite debt to TS Eliot's masterpiece *The Waste Land*, merging the voice of a disgruntled landlord ("that's it sir, you're leaving") with the hope of religious transcendence and redemption ("God loves his children").

We're still in Bowie territory on 'Subterranean Homesick Alien', hinting at the exiled spaceman Major Tom of 'Space Oddity' (cf 'Planet Telex') and also Bowie's character in the 1976 movie *The Man Who Fell To Earth*, about an alien stranded on our world. But the title is also an obvious nod to Bob Dylan's 'Subterranean Homesick Blues' (on the 1965 album *Bringing It All Back Home*), probably the first song to graft surreal, stream-of-consciousness lyrics onto a rock 'n' roll beat. It's the most specifically 'spacey' of the album's science-fiction inflected tracks, with guitars that either twinkle like stars or soar like comets. There are further literary references: "Up above aliens hover making home movies" could have been culled from the so-called 'Martian poetry' of writers like Craig Raine, who tried to view humanity from a completely objective, un-earthbound perspective: and the wish to be abducted by aliens (and then not believed) is an inversion of Whitley Strieber's supposedly true-life tale of being snatched by extra-terrestrials, *Communion*.

'Exit Music (For A Film)', as the title suggests, was specifically written for William Shakespeare's *Romeo & Juliet*, Baz Luhrmann's deconstruction of the best-known love story in the world. Thom had been listening to Johnny Cash's *Live From Folsom Prison*, and achieved the frightening echo on his voice by recording in the cavernous entrance hall of St Catherine's Court. It's a song about the fears of childhood and escaping an abusive parent, although "everlasting peace" implies that the escape is to death rather than a place of refuge. The song forms a thematic whole with the next track, 'Let Down', with its Peter Pan references ("I am going to grow wings") and the sounds of the prehistoric personal computers that all the band members used as children.

With 'Karma Police' we see yet another example of Radiohead's ability to disguise the most depressing sentiments in the form of soothing, radio-friendly rock. The Eastern concept of karma, where a person's sins return to haunt him/her, is expressed in terms of a quasi-fascist paramilitary organisation, busting people on the say-so of the neurotic narrator. The idea of a crime returning to haunt the perpetrator is also expressed in the disturbing video, directed by Jonathan Glazer. A man chased by a car retaliates by lighting a match that blows the car up. The most troubling aspect is that the camera is inside the car: the viewer is first implicated in the unexplained pursuit of the man, and is then punished when the tables are turned.

The complaint "he talks in maths" can be seen as a reference to the next track, spoken by Thom through a Macintosh voice synthesiser (although some listeners have assumed this is the artificial voice of Professor Stephen Hawking). 'Fitter Happier' is the oddest recording made by the band up to this point, being a poem with occasional sound effects hovering in the background. It makes a clever transition from the everyday banalities of modern life ("regular exercise at the gym") to the psychic agony that this causes ("a pig in a cage on antibiotics"). Thom later explained to *Rolling Stone*'s David Sinclair how he assembled the words for the track. "I bought a whole load of those how-to-improve your life books, and we'd be trying to use them in various different ways. One said something like, 'You will never make any friends unless you like everyone, genuinely.' Oh well, I'm fucked then, aren't I? And the legacy of these books goes on. You still meet people who really believe that the way to success is to adopt that smile and that smile will sell: 'Unless you believe in the product, you will not sell the product.'"

Unfortunately, the bravest experiment on the album is followed by the most run-of-the-mill rock song, 'Electioneering', the Beatlesy guitar lines of which might have passed muster as an Oasis b-side, but seem horribly outdated here. Only on the blazing fretboard throttling that forms the outro, does the song come to life - and that's a throwback to the Velvet Underground tributes of *Pablo Honey*. It's a double shame because Thom comes up with some of his most biting, politically explicit lyrics to date, encompassing "voodoo economics" (a reference to the US Presidential candidate Ross Perot) and the power of the International Monetary Fund. This would become a continuing theme in Thom's interviews.

The most unsettling track on the album is also the most domestic. 'Climbing Up The Walls' is dragged into existence on a bed of echoing drums and hamfisted bass synthesisers, and we're face to face with the domestic invader glimpsed in 'Just' - but this time Thom isn't simply describing him, he's actually singing from his point of view. Gentle childhood images ("tuck the kids in safe tonight", "toys in the basement") are contrasted with the horrifying ("open up your skull, I'll be there"). There are echoes of Robert Bloch's short story, *Enoch*, in which a serial killer blames his crimes on a mysterious entity that lives inside his head and feeds on his victim's brains. The Bloch link is carried on in the outro, as discordant violins echo the screen version of his most famous story, *Psycho*. As Jonny said to the *NME*'s Stuart Bailie: "It's the most frightening sound, like insects or something. But it's beautiful."

From sheer terror to a moment of respite, as a gentle glockenspiel heralds 'No Surprises'. We're back to the idyllic scenario of '(Nice Dream)' ("such a pretty house, such a pretty garden") but this time it's not a dreamy retreat from reality, it's a resignation, a surrender. "I'll take a quiet life," Thom sighs, and we remember that most of the band members are approaching their thirtieth birthdays, the age at which people are supposed to give up this childish rock 'n' roll lark and knuckle down to suburban oblivion.

If 'Lucky' sounded slightly moody amidst the Britpop and electronica of the *Help!* album, it's positively upbeat in the context of *OK Computer*. The overall sci-fi theme also gives a different resonance to the aircrash image - is it a bog-standard plane crash, or some kind of alien craft that's come down to earth? As with all the tracks, explicit meaning is the last thing we'll find.

'The Tourist' comes as something of an anticlimax. An attack on American tourists who zoom around Europe without giving themselves any time to experience the places they're visiting (the if-it's-Tuesday-this-must-be-Belgium scenario), its concerns seem a little petty when compared with the emotional, political and extra-terrestrial issues covered elsewhere on the album. A reflective, bluesy tune, it ends with the sound of a simple, old-fashioned receptionist's bell.

The most casual listener could deduce that *OK Computer* marked a profound change for Radiohead. They were no longer just an indie band as such, paying homage to the old reliables like Elvis Costello or The Smiths (although both were still a profound influence). Thom admitted that Miles Davis's jazz-rock masterpiece *Bitches Brew* was an influence, as well as various dance records.

The record company now trusted them not to screw up, as well. With almost total control over the sound of their records (Godrich's role was to put their ideas into practice, not to act as some kind of dominant presence behind the glass) Radiohead could fully break away from the accepted thinking of how to make a rock album.

It was a similar scenario with the visuals, Stanley Donwood worked on the sleeve again, producing a bleak series of collages based on a cold, white-dominated palette, but the band members were involved at all stages of production. Apart from the lyrics, and twisted abstracts of religious and technological images, the cover booklet is peppered with the nightmarish cartoon people that would become identified with Donwood's work for the band. There are also several snippets of text, including patches of Greek, and several words in the international language Esperanto. The design matched the music, in offering no coherent meaning, but instead a general feeling of sadness and dislocation, leaving a product that, in Donwood's understated opinion, "is quite unsettling".

This concentration on the mood of the music, rather than the literal meaning, persisted in the promos. The video for 'Paranoid Android', created by the Swedish director Magnus Carllson, featured his animated character Robin, whose blank-faced helicopter journey fits with the feel of the song, but not necessarily the lyrics. Hardly surprising, since Carllson wasn't supplied with a lyric sheet...

According to Phil Selway, "When we delivered the album to Capitol, their first reaction was, more or less, 'Commercial suicide'." But when the press reviews started trickling in, the official reaction soon changed.

James Oldham in the *NME* gave it an all-but unprecedented 10 out of 10, describing it as "both age-defining and one of the most startling albums ever made", "a spectacular success" and "one of the greatest albums of living memory". *Q*'s David Kavanagh called it "an emotionally draining, epic experience," announcing that "Radiohead can definitely be ranked high among the world's greatest bands." Mark Kemp in *Rolling Stone* warned his more conservative readers that "*OK Computer* is not an easy listen" but that, with perseverance, it was revealed "a stunning art-rock tour de force". And this was from one of the few Americans who hadn't liked 'Creep'.

So what was it that had changed? Two years before, Radiohead had seemed out of kilter with the music landscape, even a throwback to the self-destructive gloom of the early 1990s. Now they were being hailed as the band that could sum up all of modern society in the space of an hour. *Select*'s John Harris (the man who'd told On A Friday to change their name in 1992), explained the shift, at least in terms of the UK. In May, Tony Blair's Labour Party had won the General Election, utterly crushing the Conservative Party that had held sway for 18 long years. As the backward-looking Tories were consigned to the scrapheap, so the nostalgic, IY1966 music that had dominated the last few years would follow it.

This might have been a little unfair on acts like Oasis, who had publicly backed Tony Blair long before he entered Downing Street, but the release of their third album, *Be Here Now*, a few months after *OK Computer*, revealed that their inspiration was pretty much exhausted. In John Harris's words, "we are in need of a truly modern kind of rock". Like Mark Kemp, he acknowledged that "it needs five or six plays before you even begin to understand it," but, the implication was, it's worth it. Or, as Sam Steele concluded in *Vox*, "Radiohead are paying no attention to polite convention. They are cruising on warp factor ten, trailing sleighbells, synthesisers, whole bloody choirs of angels, and an entire neo-Freudian thesis in their wake."

But this need for a new start wasn't confined to their home country. Joseph Patel, in the US-based *Wall Of Sound* e-zine, described the album as "a brilliantly imaginative piece that will infallibly erase the horrid memories of fellow UK exports Bush and Oasis". There seemed to be a universal need for a band that would take risks, that would take rock music seriously - a band that was prepared to mean something. And Radiohead had fulfilled that need.

A few days after the release of *OK Computer*, Radiohead played a set at the Glastonbury Festival, translating the complex, unfamiliar grooves of the album to a soggy, mud-caked crowd. Despite the PA and the lights both failing, it was a transcendent performance, confirming that Radiohead were back on top of their game, expressing the emotions of an entire generation. It was similar to the buzz that had been created by 'Creep', four years before, but multiplied by a thousand. And that wasn't necessarily a development that the band would welcome.

# CHAPTER 8

# THE TOURIST

*"I have such a low boredom threshold that I need something
more than good songs to keep my attention."*
*Jonny Greenwood*

*"We have a choice: we may try to understand, or refuse to do so,
contributing to the likelihood that much worse lies ahead."*
*Noam Chomsky*

Radiohead weren't just flavour of the month among critics, they
were a hot commercial property again. *OK Computer*
topped the UK album charts (it just missed the Top
20 in the US) and the three singles it spawned
(*Paranoid Android*, *Karma Police* and *No Surprises*)
all reached the British Top 10. There was no single
song that dominated the summer in the manner that
'Creep' had done - instead, 1997 was the year of *OK
Computer* in the way that 1967 had been the year
of *Sergeant Pepper's Lonely Hearts Club Band* - it
had gone beyond the level of an album to become
some sort of cultural signifier, an artifact that could
be used to sum up a historical moment. And the
band were no longer the exclusive property of post-
grunge slackers or sensitive, middle-class students
who'd been unlucky in love. *OK Computer* was a
soundtrack in wine bars and shoe shops, driving music,
soundtrack fodder. It was part of the landscape. In 1993
their appearance amidst the toned tits of an MTV
babefest was an incongruous culture clash. In 1997 their
US tour was topped and tailed by spots on the most high-
profile American TV shows. In July they performed
'Electioneering' on Jay Leno's *Tonight Show*, and the
following month David Letterman's *Late Show* was
the setting for a rendition of 'Karma Police'. And
the weirdest thing was how un-weird the whole
thing seemed. The hip irony of their appearance
alongside smooth-talking frontmen like Leno and
Letterman showed a blurring of categories and
distinctions, to the extent that Radiohead were no
longer simply trailblazers for 'indie' or 'alternative' or
'college rock'. They were, quite simply, the biggest,
most high-profile band in the world. In fact, by 1998,

*Q* magazine had labelled *OK Computer* the greatest album of all time. After less than 18 months it was not only being ranked alongside the seminal offerings of The Beatles, Bowie and Pink Floyd, it was leaving them choking in the dust.

This would be a heavy responsibility for anyone to bear, but for a character as hypersensitive and prickly as Thom Yorke it was all but unbearable. To add to the pressure, the promotional jamboree that followed the album's release was covered by a film crew, making the documentary that would later be released as *Meeting People Is Easy*. Pretty soon the band members were turning into paranoid androids, and it all came to a head in November when they played a soulless mega-shed called the National Exhibition Centre, in Birmingham.

As Thom later told *Rolling Stone*'s David Fricke: "I came off at the end of that show, sat in the dressing room and couldn't speak... I'd just so had enough. And I was bored with saying I'd had enough. I was beyond that."

Thom had reached the impasse faced by many icons of existentialism and nihilism. If you build your career on world-weariness, what happens when even that makes you weary? Numbness, nothingness, what Fricke described as "mute, vengeful paralysis".

There were some fun distractions. Through their friendship with REM's Michael Stipe they became involved in working on the soundtrack of a movie directed by Todd Haynes, *Velvet Goldmine*. A fictionalised version of the rise to fame of David Bowie and Iggy Pop, it had mixed fortunes at the box office and at the hands of the critics; but Stipe, as executive producer, managed to pull in several of his friends from the music industry to ensure that at least the music worked. Jonny and Thom were lined up alongside former members of Suede, Grant Lee Buffalo and Roxy Music to create the fictional combo Venus In Furs (a name borrowed from the Velvet Underground song). Most of the tracks were reworkings of Roxy Music songs from the early 70s, and Thom acquired much praise for his accurate mimickry of Roxy frontman Bryan Ferry.

But there was still the old touring treadmill. January saw the band touring in Japan, followed by gigs in Australia and New Zealand. In the midst of this, *OK Computer* was awarded the Grammy for 'Best Alternative Music Performance', whatever that might mean. Prizes such as this put Radiohead in a difficult position. On the one hand, they've got nothing but contempt for the glitzy, back-slapping, PR-driven side of the music industry. Why should they care if an anonymous bunch of industry insiders want to label their latest CD as the least unacceptable example of post-punk guitar torture in the last twelve months? On the other hand, the band's continued success, in fact its survival, was dependent on that very industry, on

a big capitalist institution called EMI, also responsible for selling the output of such cutting edge artists as Paul McCartney, Cliff Richard and Queen. If Radiohead were to turn round and slag off the music business and all it stood for, they'd rightly be seen as hypocrites, biting the well-manicured hand that fed them. They were in a political and economic double-bind, and something had to give.

Of course, there had been political rock acts before. However, they tended to fall into two categories. The deeply committed ones (Rage Against The Machine, Dead Kennedys, Public Enemy, Billy Bragg) never seemed to achieve the success they deserved; either they tore themselves apart trying to balance political and musical concerns, or the punters grew weary of their preaching and they faded away. The other kind is the hugely successful star who stumbles into activism more through boredom than anything else: John Lennon's early-70s flirtations with Maoism and David Bowie's coked-up Führer complex a few years later spring to mind.

But there were performers who were able to balance political commitment with a successful career. U2, REM and the Beastie Boys had used their success to draw their fans' attention to a number of thorny issues, such as debt relief and the Chinese occupation of Tibet. Of course, some observers argued that by remaining part of the capitalist profit system, the bands were contributing to such problems. And others felt that becoming interested in an issue just because your favourite pop star mentioned it in his sleeve notes was a pretty shallow form of political engagement. Which is probably so, but surely it's better than nothing.

Thom had for some time been interested in the works of Noam Chomsky, a writer and thinker on all aspects of politics, but especially US foreign and economic policy. In recent years, especially after the fall of communism and the rise of the USA to become the undisputed world superpower, Chomsky's views had taken root in a number of campaigns, such as the fight against the introduction of genetically-modified food, or to improve condition in Asian sweatshops producing branded sports goods for companies like Nike. Although these were mostly single-issue campaigns, there was a common thread, a resistance to the international network of political and economic power that had been dubbed globalisation. Huge, unaccountable bodies like the International Monetary Fund and the World Trade Organization suddenly found that their meetings were being disrupted by protesters. People who took on a big corporate company, like the London activists who sued McDonald's, found that supporters from all over the world would come to their aid. Suddenly it felt as if there was a genuine mood for change, a desire to kick over the old statues.

But how to do it? Anti-globalisation protestors were often criticised for failing to come up with a coherent alternative: the spoof collective Cyderdelic summed up the problem best with their slogan "Smash Capitalism And Replace It With Something Nicer". But there was no doubt that a generation that had given up on the orthodox political process weren't prepared to swallow the undiluted effluent of big business any more. And there were always accusations of hypocrisy. In 2000, when Naomi Klein brought out *No Logo*, her diatribe against the big brands (Nike, Coca-Cola, Gap etc), cynics pointed out that 'No Logo' itself had become a trendy logo. Moreover the success of the book was partly down to the marketing power of its publishers, Harper Collins, an arm of the mighty Rupert Murdoch empire, criticized for being soft on the Chinese tyrants occupying Tibet... and so it goes on. Anything could be interpreted as selling out, as Thom was prepared to admit: "I'm as confused as anybody, you know what I mean? I've got no idea, absolutely no idea. I mean, I was wearing Nike in the 'Just' video."

So, what could Radiohead do? Turning their songs into explicit slogans wasn't their style, and neither was the in-your-face complaining perfected by the likes of Bob Geldof and U2's Bono, bullying high-profile world leaders like Margaret Thatcher and Pope John Paul II to get their cases across. Thom and the others discussed their ideas in interviews, but they were wary of preaching - why were their views more important than anyone else's, just because they were musicians? They weren't averse to lending their names to a good cause (their contribution to *Help!* was an artistic success, as well as a charitable deed) and played several benefit concerts in the months after *OK Computer* was released.

Thom was prepared to stand up for what he believed in, even if it meant associating himself with the more respectable, showbizzy side of politics. "Personally, I was really happy to get involved in Jubilee 2000," he told Lauren Zoric of *The Guardian*, "because it is a mainstream, acceptable face of resistance against the antics of the IMF and the World Bank."

On the other hand, he also put himself on the line by attending some of the anti-globalisation protests that were springing up around the world. "The protests themselves are pretty nasty affairs. I went on the one in London, and there were so-called undercover guys walking around in bullet-proof jackets with long-lens cameras, and two armed bodyguards, walking through the crowd taking photos of 'troublemakers' - that basically meant everybody in Trafalgar Square." He has no trouble in reconciling the two wings of the movement, because the ends, in his view, justify the means. "I am interested in the unacceptable face of it, in terms of the media coverage, the disruptive elements, the anarchists, because I don't really care what methods are used to make the IMF and World Bank so unpopular that they dismantle it. I don't really care how it happens, as long as it happens. That's the point."

One particularly important issue to the band was the situation in Tibet. In 1959, China had invaded the country, sending the religious ruler, the Dalai Lama into exile and attempting to eradicate the Tibetans' language, culture and religion. To add to the problem, media tycoons like Rupert Murdoch maintained major interests in China, which meant that it was increasingly difficult to keep the situation in the public eye.

After their successful US tour, supported by Spiritualized, Radiohead leant their support to the Tibet Freedom Concert, due to be held in Washington DC on June 13, 1998. In the event, a heavy rainstorm caused the cancellation of the gig, and Radiohead decamped to the nearby 9.30 club, where they played an impromptu set, with Pulp in support, and onstage assistance from REM's Michael Stipe. When the Tibet gig was restaged the following day,

the bands collaborated again, Stipe singing on 'Lucky' and Thom providing vocals on two REM numbers. Then, on June 15, an acoustic concert was staged opposite the Capitol, at which the band played 'Street Spirit'.

After the concert, Thom expressed his frustration that his views were given extra consideration simply because he was a 'celebrity'. "I don't think it's a legitimate role, I think it's fucking ridiculous that we're the only people allowed to do it," he raged in an interview for *Raygun* magazine. "I think it's a fucking farce, because we're not that informed, you have to make such a huge effort. Surely you think someone who gets paid to be a politician would be better informed than you. But it's in their interests to keep you uninformed. That's fucked."

But what Radiohead were seeking wasn't simply a pile of political brownie points. Ending Third World debt or cutting back pollution were all well and good, but they were just symptoms of a deeper malaise. *OK Computer*, with its multiple points of view, had demonstrated that the band were interested in looking at lyrical concerns from different angles - now maybe it was time to go deeper, to take a different perspective on the music itself.

Thom and his bandmates were always keen to collaborate or tour with other interesting musicians, but up to now this had mostly been restricted to the field of guitar music (recording with Sparklehorse and Drugstore, touring with REM and Belly). But, by comparison with Radiohead's first two albums, much of *OK Computer* was very different from 'rock' as the term is usually understood. As Ed said to Albert Clapps of Stereo-Type in 1997: "There wasn't any need to rock out on this record, no sort of 4-wheel drive. If people want rock they can go and listen to Aerosmith."

The real sonic progressions in the 1990s had come not from guitar acts, but in the fields of dance and electronic music. Radiohead had first dabbled here before the release of *The Bends*, with a club-directed 12-inch of 'Planet Telex' featuring remixes by Steve Osborne and LFO.

More recently they had become fascinated by the dark trip-hop of acts like Massive Attack, and Thom had provided vocals for 'Rabbit In Your Headlights', a collaboration with DJ Shadow for James Lavelle's UNKLE project. Shadow and Lavelle had supported the band on their UK tour in 1997, an early sign that purist rock fans might be disoriented by Radiohead's new directions. The lyrics to 'Rabbit In Your Headlights' could well have fitted onto any of the previous Radiohead albums; lines like "fat bloody fingers are sucking your soul away" and "Christian suburbanite washed down the toilet" proved that the supposedly hedonistic universe of dance culture could be as bleak and morbid as the land of moody guitars. The video for the track was similar in construction to the one for 'Karma Police', in that it involved a lone individual at the mercy of traffic. This time, the man is regularly knocked down by speeding cars, but, again, retribution is in the air, as the last car blows up.

But it wasn't just a question of lyrics and videos. Massive Attack and DJ Shadow, as well as performers like the Aphex Twin, µZiq (Mike Paradinas) and Atari Teenage Riot, were using the sounds and technology developed on the back of hip-hop and acid house to create unsettling, confrontational music. The music wasn't political in the sense of addressing a particular issue or criticizing a specific politician - but its refusal to play by the accepted conventions of what we call 'pop' or 'rock' made the listener think harder about the process that delivered the little shiny disc to his or her stereo.

In some ways, these bands shared a perspective with the 'free jazz' performers of the 1960s and 1970s. Musicians like Albert Ayler, Ornette Coleman and Cecil Taylor expressed their loathing for the corrupt, violent, racist environment of Nixon's America not through words but through harsh, dissonant, anti-melodic music. If jazz music, a defiantly black art form, were to be co-opted and debased by white performers and commercial record companies, these guys were going to take it back and twist it around until the suburban, white middle-classes didn't want it any more.

The traumas and inner tensions were put under the spotlight in November with the release of the documentary *Meeting People Is Easy*, in which the contrast between Thom's quietly charismatic stage persona and his troubled off-stage existence became apparent. Radiohead had one more commitment, appropriately combining their musical and political ambitions; a concert in Paris in support of the human rights organisation Amnesty International, alongside such luminaries as Bruce Springsteen, Alanis Morissette and Shania Twain. Just as it had done on the Capitol lawn in June, 'Street Spirit' closed the concert. Thom introduced the song with an inarticulate but heartfelt speech that indicated how uncomfortable he was at wearing his political heart on his sleeve.

"I know it'll probably sound corny," he said, "but this one's for everybody being mistreated by their government. That's for human rights, if anybody knows what it is. Let's hope you don't get tired of hearing about it."

And then, for a long time, the shutters went down on Radiohead.

# CHAPTER 9

KNIVES OUT

# KNIVES OUT

*"It was necessary to go away and glue back the pieces."*
*Thom Yorke*

*"A mistake repeated three times becomes an arrangement."*
*David Bowie*

1999 was pretty much a Radiohead-free zone as far as the wider world was concerned. If there were any Yorkean words of wisdom to be dissected, they probably came from Thom's younger brother Andy, whose band The Unbelievable Truth were making serious waves. Their first album, *Almost Here*, had been released the previous year, and, while not as groundbreaking as his elder, Andy was proving to be a sensitive, imaginative songwriter. Unfortunately, the music press being what it is, journalists were always keener to delve into Andy's family background than to talk about the music, and record label problems, plus a dispute with an ex-manager, pushed The Unbelievable Truth into oblivion in 2000.

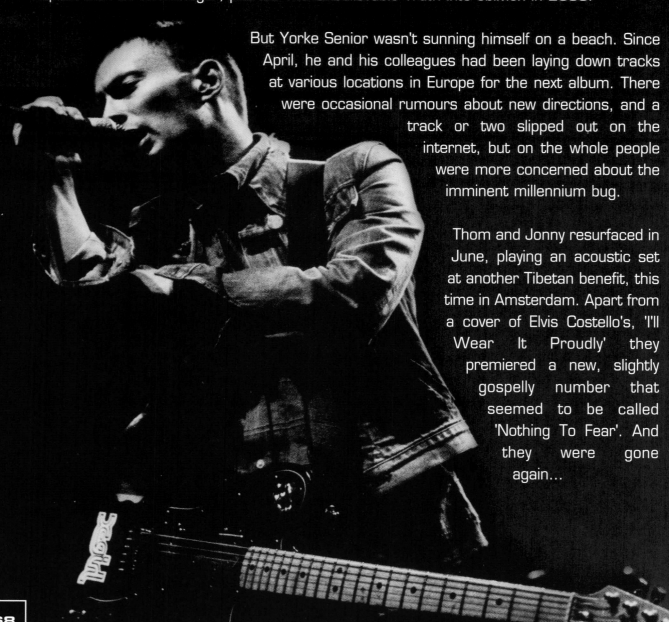

But Yorke Senior wasn't sunning himself on a beach. Since April, he and his colleagues had been laying down tracks at various locations in Europe for the next album. There were occasional rumours about new directions, and a track or two slipped out on the internet, but on the whole people were more concerned about the imminent millennium bug.

Thom and Jonny resurfaced in June, playing an acoustic set at another Tibetan benefit, this time in Amsterdam. Apart from a cover of Elvis Costello's, 'I'll Wear It Proudly' they premiered a new, slightly gospelly number that seemed to be called 'Nothing To Fear'. And they were gone again...

...until December, when Johny and Thom went into a studio and did a live webcast of the first new Radiohead material for nearly two years. And just to prove that Radiohead weren't going to join in the party mood as the world looked forward to the next century, it was a song about cannibalism. Lovely.

The band faded from sight yet again, until June 2000, when they staged a relatively low-key gig in the French town of Arles. The songs they played that night were unlike anything the audience had heard before. Keyboard drones, odd time signatures, incoherent lyrics – Radiohead had used these techniques before, but not as the basis for entire songs.

Hardcore fans began taping these new songs, and more tracks were being downloaded from the internet. Details began to come out about the new material. No singles. No videos. A double album... or would it be two albums released at once? Would one of them be instrumental? Dance mixes? Nothing but white noise?

What had they been up to? Ed O'Brien later explained the scenario to Zev Borow of *Spin*: "Musically, I think we all came to it a bit vague. Thom didn't know exactly what he wanted the new record to be either, but he did know what he didn't want it to be, which was anything that smacked of the old route, or of being a rock'n'roll band. He's got a low boredom threshold and is very good at giving us a kick up the ass. But at the same time, sometimes you need a softer approach.

"The initial sessions of *Kid A* were really sort of make-or-break for us as a band. We had to think long and hard about whether we wanted to continue at all. For me, at least, it was about growing up. If there was a trade-off, my bottom line was I was not willing to become a completely inept asshole for the sake of the music."

So we had a meeting, and there was a scary, unspoken sort of fear. We were really serious. I mean, why not go out on top? But we've known each other for 15 years, and here we are now just getting to the point where we can do things the way we want. So now it's like, we're going to make mistakes, but let's retain a degree of calmness."

Disaster averted, and with a slightly more cohesive idea of what they wanted from the sessions, the band had spent the next few months at studios in Denmark, France and Germany, as well as their base in Oxford, throwing all their ideas together. But it still wasn't clear to the outside world what those ideas actually sounded like...

Thom later explained the process to the Japanese journalist Yoichiri Yamasaki: "A lot of the songwriting now isn't really about songwriting at all, it's about editing, building up a lot of material, then piecing it together like a painter." It was clear this wasn't just going to be So

In September the band put their 'anti-corporate' policies into practice, bypassing big urban arenas and staging their UK tour in their own portable tent. Any other act might have used this as an excuse for circus or fairground-related imagery, but Radiohead's new songs didn't exactly lend themselves to that sort of treatment. *OK Computer* might not have been party music, but there were some doubts that the new stuff could be characterised as music at all.

Also, the band's refusal to go on the promotional merry-go-round came in for some criticism. As Andrew Collins put it in *Q*, "By refusing to step out from behind their kooky photos and say 'this is me' Thom Yorke and co are pandering to the very rock 'n' roll mythmaking process they claim to deplore."

But it was the music that was going to count. Finally, October 2000 saw Radiohead's first new album in over three years, although apparently there was at least another album's worth in the can. It was called *Kid A*, a reference to the identity of the world's first cloned human - a child who, in Thom's view, already existed.

Expectation was intense, and, whatever the fans might have thought when first listening to the album, that intensity was justified. Pretty electric piano opens the account, on 'Everything In Its Right Place' - a title saturated with irony. Everything is completely out of place, as the tune is gradually overrun by buzzing tapes and a heavily synthesised voice insisting "Yesterday I woke up sucking a lemon." This is a possible analogy for the whole listening experience - it hurts like hell but it probably does you some kind of good. More grinding vocals and sampled, found sound merge with rainwater-like keyboard notes on the title track. Listen closely and you can just about make out the lyrics "rats and children follow me out of town," a clear reference to the legendary Pied Piper of Hamlin. This odd character supposedly lured away the rats that had infested a German town through the power of his music. But when the inhabitants failed to pay him for his troubles, he did the same thing to their children. The Piper is a clear precursor to the Rock Star As Messiah idea exploited so brilliantly by Bowie and with which Thom Yorke is profoundly uneasy.

By this stage, the listener is disoriented, grabbing for straws, and in this inverted universe the sound of a real, identifiable instrument comes as something of a relief. Colin's funky bass figure, quickly joined by Phil's Stone Roses-like drums, anchor 'The National Anthem', and we seem to be approaching something like a conventional pop song. At least, we are until a small battalion of jazz saxophonists (including members of the Borneo Horns, who played with Bowie in the mid-80s) let rip. At first, the mournful honking suggests a New Orleans funeral choir, but the ghosts of Albert Ayler and John Coltrane sprinkle their freeform stardust over the whole ensemble and the track turns into a juggernaut of uncontrolled improvisation. This is the jazz they don't play on Jazz FM, people. Not niiice. Somewhere in amongst the squawking beauty, Thom burbles "Everyone has got the fear," and, for the first time, you know pretty much what he means. This is threatening music, harnessing the incendiary rage of free jazz to what's supposed to be a pop song. As the track fades we hear a snippet of something that might well be a real national anthem, but it's so blurry, it's hard to say. And by this stage, who cares about the 'real' national anthem?

'How To Disappear Completely' is the oldest song here, written in Toronto in 1997 and first performed live on the American tour the following year. It's also the most conventional - the first time on the album that you can hear an identifiable guitar sound. But the acoustic strumming that wouldn't have seemed out of place on *Pablo Honey* is edged out by tortured strings and a lyric that seems to hint at the inner torment of someone like Richey Edwards. "In a little while I'll be gone," implies suicide but doesn't say it, playing with euphemisms about death and identity. It could just be a note to let your mum know you're going down to the shops. The banal and the horrific lie side by side, and we don't know the difference. Next, the sustained notes of 'Treefingers' provide the first pure instrumental on any Radiohead album. But by this stage, words are of secondary importance to the physical feel of the album - this was the first album since *Pablo Honey* not to have the lyrics printed on the packaging.

When Radiohead come up with something called 'Optimistic,' the most casual observer would probably guess the song was anything but. Clanging guitars and faintly ominous tom-toms propel a lyric that covers flies, vultures, fish and dinosaurs, a breakneck tour around the nastier side of nature. "I'd really like to help you, man," but it's a dog-eat-dog world. High-pitched 'woo-woos' allude to 'Sympathy For The Devil', the Rolling Stones at their most feral. Somewhere in here, Jonny is supposedly playing the Ondes Martinot, a bizarre electronic instrument invented in the 1920s that prefigured the modern synthesiser.

We jump abruptly to guitar lines that sound like The Beatles' 'Here Comes The Sun' with Tourette's syndrome. We're 'In Limbo' a 'fantasy world' where any potential happiness can be lost through a cynically situated trapdoor. We're in the same territory as '(Nice Dream)' and 'No Surprises', a superficially idyllic existence that's really anything but.

'Idioteque' enters on the back of samples from avant-garde electronic music from the 1970s, sounding for all the world like a human beatbox with asthma. We descend from the noble, altruistic cry of "women and children first" to "the first of the children," an allusion to the slaughters of the first-born in the Bible. In surroundings like these, "I'll laugh until my head comes off" should be taken literally, not figuratively. In the distance, a door creaks.

Children don't come off any better as we segue to the next track, 'Morning Bell'. Over a bed of shuffling, sampled drums and synthesised vibes, kids are cut in half and Thom pleads "release me!" And release is at hand in 'Motion Picture Soundtrack', even if you need to get it via a cocktail of "red wine and sleeping pills", a return to the suicide and oblivion motifs of 'How To Disappear Completely'. Jonny shows his extraordinary versatility here, doubling on moody church organ and lush harp. In an ironic acknowledgement of being dubbed 'the greatest band in the world ever', there seems to be a triple acknowledgement of the previous holders of that title, The Beatles: the overblown, neo-classical arrangement harks back to 'Good Night', the closing song on *The Beatles* (aka *The White Album*); then there's a long gap (as at the end of Abbey Road); and the album closes with a burst of abstract noise, just like *Sergeant Pepper's Lonely Hearts Club Band.*

Once more, Stanley Donwood provided his characteristically inscrutable, eerie designs. The cover echoes the Ice Age imagery of 'Idioteque' but was also taken by some to represent the mountain that listeners had to climb if they wanted to get into Radiohead's new sound.

Of course, *OK Computer* hadn't been the sort of album to grab listeners by the ears and bellow "love me!" But this was uneasy listening and then some. In spades. With a cherry on top. The best analysis that *Rolling Stone*'s David Fricke could summon up was "If you're looking for instant joy and easy definition, you are swimming in the wrong soup." This was "a work of deliberately inky, almost irritating obsession." But what he couldn't decide was whether it was any good or not.

Similarly non-commital was the *NME*, calling the album a "patently magnificent construct" but making slighting remarks about the title track ("sub-Aphex Twin doodling") and 'Motion Picture Soundtrack' ("a sorely anticlimactic closer") that gave quite the opposite picture. In fact, the songs that meet with most favour are those, like 'How To Disappear Completely', that stick most closely to conventional rock structures and instrumentation.

Simon Reynolds of *Spin* was more positive, however, concluding that "the fans will persevere and discover that *Kid A* is not only Radiohead's bravest album but its best one as well."

This was tough stuff, a record for discerning listeners. *OK Computer* had done well, but that was still basically a rock album. *Kid A* was dense, messy, experimental, a record designed to be influential rather than popular, thought-provoking rather than loveable. As Stuart Maconie put it in *Q*, "*Kid A* will still baffle and upset those who are disappointed that they don't do 'Creep' anymore." The lyrics reach new levels of abstract unpleasantness, although it's possible to read too much into the words. In his interview with Yamasaki, Thom explained: "All the stuff I've been listening to, almost none of it has vocals. That was one of the things that I was most interested in; that I was so in love with this music, yet there wasn't much vocal interpretation... You're not supposed to think about the words. That's the whole point all through the record. That's why I'm not printing the lyrics. Never. Maybe I'll give people clues, but it shouldn't be read like that. That's how it works out. With 'Everything In Its Right Place', when you actually read the lyrics, if I wrote them out, they're just really silly. "Yesterday I woke up sucking a lemon." That's pretty silly. But I thought it was funny when I sang it. When I listened to it afterwards, it meant something else."

As with *The Bends*, Capitol, Radiohead's US record company, had been slightly flummoxed by the new album. Supposedly, company president Roy Lott ordered his LA sales staff to drive to Malibu beach while listening to *Kid A*, to help them get their heads round it. And when it hit the top of the charts on both sides of the Atlantic, jaws dropped in all departments. After the event, Lott claimed to *Spin* magazine that he'd been behind the album all the way. "I had no expectations of what the record would or should sound like," he said. "Is it a challenge for us? Sure. But the record is great. In fact, the analogy that comes to mind is the Beach Boys' *Pet Sounds*, and we still sell a lot of those..."

Essentially, nervous industry insiders had reckoned without the record-buying public's expectations of Radiohead. If you buy a record by Thom and the boys, you know you're in for something challenging and worthwhile. As producer Nigel Godrich put it: "If Oasis made a record like this, I don't think anybody would go for it. But, you know, it isn't something to put on at a dinner party... I don't really expect people to like it."

The band had refused to release videos for the album, but they did make a few TV appearances, culminating in a surreal slot on the American satire *Saturday Night Live*. Performing 'The National Anthem' and 'Idioteque' on the show that had spawned the likes of John Belushi, Chris Rock and Adam Sandler might not have seemed the most natural juxtaposition, but why expect the expected from these guys? As Thom said afterwards: "For me it was like being a child and somebody saying, "You have ten minutes of television in America, completely live, no gaps, and you can do whatever the fuck you like and there will be X millions of people watching!"

*Kid A* was placed strongly in the music press end-of-year roundups, most notably in *Spin* magazine, where the Readers' Poll gave Radiohead  the top slot for Best Artist, Best Live Act, Best Song ('Optimistic'), Best Album and best *Spin* cover. Thom even made it to second place, along with Christina Aguilera, in the 'Sex God And Goddess' rankings, losing out only to the inspired combination of Trent Reznor and Britney Spears.

Radiohead were back, entirely on their own terms. And, amazingly, there was more where that came from.

# CHAPTER 10

KINETIC

*The first time I heard it I thought it was the most nauseating chaos.*
*Thom Yorke on Miles Davis's Bitches Brew*

Some people like structure, order, predictability. They like films with a good story, pictures of something you can recognise, and comfortable, sensible trousers that don't wear out round the crotch. And some people like their rock bands to do the same. They like them to release a single (with a video), then release an album (with the single on it again), then go on tour (during which they'll release another single from the album), then, after the tour, rest for a few weeks and go back into the studio.

Radiohead, as you may have gathered, don't play it that way. With *Kid A*, they'd disembowelled the idea of The Rock Song. As Thom said to *Select* magazine: "It seems music has got to a point where everybody has the right to go to a place they like. And it shouldn't be over your career or one record. It can be over one song or half a song, or even ten seconds. There's ten seconds of hip-hop on the LP, y'know. To me, that's how I listen to music now. I don't want to be in a rock band any more, anyway."

This disjointed process of music-making had created an embarrassment of riches. During the sessions that spawned *Kid A*, they'd recorded many more tunes, enough to form a coherent album on its own. The critical consensus was that the next album, nicknamed 'Kid B' in the press, would be more straightforward, with proper guitar solos and tunes you could whistle. Thom's claim that the band warmed up by playing post-punk and indie classics by the likes of Magazine and The Smiths added to the 'classic rock' rumours.

Meanwhile, fans of the band were in two minds about a 'tribute' paid by two Radio One DJs, Mark Radcliffe and Marc 'Lard' Riley, in the guise of The Shirehorses, who had recorded a track called 'No Big Sizes' on their second album. Moreover, the record in question was called *Our Kid Eh*, and the sleeve was a parody of *Kid A*'s mountain design, twisted into a Lowryesque cityscape. Mark and Lard were possibly hoping for some sort of reaction from Radiohead's devoted admirers (not known for having a wacky sense of humour) but, in a way, the release was a genuine salute to the band's success. For a supposedly uncommercial, experimental, all-but-tune-free album to be so successful that punters can recognise a piss-take of it, it has to have seeped into the consciousness of the buying public.

So, inevitably, *Amnesiac* had a tough act to follow. The packaging, as ever, set the tone, one of Stanley Donwood's inky cartoon beings adorning a battered, red cloth-bound book. Exorcising some classroom trauma from Abingdon days, or an excuse for a lame joke? (As

And, with the opening track, we're defiantly in Radiohead territory. The electric piano intro echoes 'Everything In Its Right Place', the first track on *Kid A*, and it's not the last time that there will be a direct link with *Amnesiac*'s predecessor. Over a clicky, nervous techno beat comes a pulse of clanging industrial noise. Something is 'Packt (sic) Like Sardines In A Crushd (sic) Tin Box', but what? Is this an allusion to the transport of veal calves, the trains to the Nazi concentration camps, or just to suburban commuter hell. As Thom mumbles "I'm a reasonable man" like a slightly paranoid *Daily Mail* reader, maybe it's the latter?

Next comes the song originally labelled 'Nothing To Fear', premiered in an acoustic version at the Tibet concert in Amsterdam nearly two years before. Now called 'Pyramid Song' and released as the first single from *Amnesiac*, it begins as a gospel-inflected ("I jumped in the river and what did I see?") lament with a doomy piano backing, before picking up stumbling, out-of-synch drums and slabs of orchestral noise. "And we all went to heaven in a little rowing boat" is a direct quotation from 'The Clapping Song', recorded by Shirley Ellis in 1965 and covered by The Belle Stars 17 years later.

Clanking electronica, spacey noise-bursts and deformed vocals have now become as much a Radiohead trademark as gloomy ballads used to be, and 'Pulk/Pull Revolving Doors' is no exception. There's also another link, carrying over the menacing "trap door" references from 'Kid A'. 'You And Whose Army' looks back even further - its "come on, come on" intro echoes 'Karma Police' from *OK Computer*. But even on their groundbreaking third album, it's unlikely that Radiohead would have constructed a whole song based on playground taunts and chants.

'I Might Be Wrong' fulfills a similar function to 'How To Disappear Completely', a relatively conventional song that startles because it sounds so out of place in the midst of all this experimental noisemongering. It's a distorted country blues, similar to the indie/roots fusion made popular by the likes of Beck and Sparklehorse. "Let's go down the waterfall, have ourselves a good time," sings Thom, harking back yet again to the fake idylls of '(Nice Dream)' and 'In Limbo', before the song dissolves into a burst of damaged trip-hop beats.

'Knives Out' is the 'cannibalism song' webcast by Thom and Jonny in 1999, with horrific subject matter thrown into relief by the ironically banal cliché of "still there's no point in letting it go to waste". This compares with the similarly old-fashioned phrase "women and children first" in 'Idioteque' - maybe one day Thom will write an entire song based on the things old people say. Meanwhile, "I'm not coming back" covers the same suicide/oblivion territory as 'How To Disappear Completely'.

Bands are allowed to plagiarise themselves (it's called self-reference), but *Amnesiac* takes the principle to a new level by repeating an entire song from *Kid A*. 'Amnesiac/Morning Bell', as it's gently retitled here, is less fragile and neurotic than the earlier version, but the sense of despair remains.

And just when you think you're listening to a remix of Radiohead's greatest moments, they do something new. 'Dollars And Cents' is the band's first explicitly political song, taking on the identity of global antichrists like the WTO and the IMF and warning that he will "crack your little soul". Urgent, menacing strings and a busy bass line impart a real sense of the threat such organisations pose.

Like *Kid A*, there's an instrumental hiatus, the bluesy 'Hunting Bears', which sounds like a soundtrack to an American road movie. Then the bubbling gloop of primordial soup introduces 'Like Spinning Plates', the core of which is an earlier, unreleased song, 'I Will' played backwards. Radiohead move from singing about cannibalism, to doing it.

Just as the last track on *Kid A* referred back to several Beatles albums, the closer on *Amnesiac* also looks to the past. The theme ("don't talk politics and don't throw stones") goes back to the central figure in 'No Surprises', a man who's given up the political fight and retreated into bourgeois conformity. Meanwhile the dolorous, New Orleans horns (a mellow version of the frantic squawking on 'The National Anthem') echo Chet Baker's contribution to Elvis Costello's 'Shipbuilding', for which Radiohead brought in another jazz trumpet legend, Humphrey Lyttleton, whose band Colin had booked at Cambridge. Lyttleton's background has parallels with that of the Radiohead members - from a posh, Establishment background (Eton and the Grenadier Guards) he became a major player in the British traditional jazz boom of the 1950s.

*Amnesiac* can be a frustrating listen. There are some magnificent songs there, but it could be argued that it follows the pattern of *Kid A* (startling sprawls of noise terrorism, interspersed with occasional pop gems) too closely. Indeed, sometimes it seems less of a sequel or companion piece to the 2000 album - more of an indecently hasty remake. Which doesn't make it a waste, just something of a disappointment - although, if *Amnesiac* had been released first, opinions might well have been reversed.

*Amnesiac's* release saw critics as disoriented as they had been when *Kid A* came out. Having finally cottoned on to the secret of understanding the band (expect the unexpected) they realised that they hadn't known what to expect. Some rumours declared that the album would be simply 'Kid A: Part 2'; others hinted that, with all that dance and jazz malarkey out of their systems, Radiohead would write another 'Creep', or maybe even turn into U2. Reviewers had been left in a state of abject confusion, and by the time they'd spun their promo copies a few times, they were none the wiser. Victoria Segal in the *NME* discussed the "expectation that *Amnesiac* will at last reveal Radiohead's secret cache of pure-gold songs, the band stepping out of their closely guarded shadows, peeling off their techno-terrorist balaclavas and releasing the music they always really wanted to make."

But had they done this? They'd caved in by releasing singles ('Knives Out' also achieved standalone status), but there was no concession to conventional 'radio-friendly' qualities. What Radiohead had done with *Kid A* was to change the rules of engagement about what rock music sounds like. *Amnesiac* was equally left-field, but because it was released in the shadow of its predecessor, it seemed less extrordinary. And, as Jon Pareles put it in *Rolling Stone*, "they have gone on to dismantle whatever they might have taken for granted about songs themselves." Only Sasha Frere-Jones, himself an avant-garde musician with the New York trio Ui, refused to be awed at Radiohead's courage. "Resonant, dusty somethings, not much on their own, line up and aggregate into something fluid and sweetly steady," he argued in *Spin*. It wasn't that this was a bad album, but Thom was compared to George W Bush: "Both mollify their fans by mumbling endless variations on 'I don't know'. Both lend trifles weight by draaaawwwing theeem ouuutt." David Stubbs, in *Uncut*, was far more positive, dubbing Radiohead as the only true inheritors of the cutting-edge music of Elvis Costello, The Fall and Joy Division. "One day soon, the likes of Radiohead may well indeed disappear completely," he concluded, "and then the world, though it doesn't know it, will be sorry".

The intensity of production might have exhausted a normal band, but Radiohead had dozens of live engagements to fulfil before the end of 2001, covering Europe, North America and Japan. But the most significant to the band was their return to Oxford in July, a majestic two-hour set in rain-sodden South Park. And, to make it a proper homecoming, the encore was a startling, but entirely appropriate rendition of 'Creep', the song that they'd claimed to loathe. "This is clearly a band aiming for visceral garage-rock rather than cerebral avant-jazz" decided Stephen Dalton in the *NME*. Had Radiohead finally got it all out of their system?

EXIT MUSIC

# EXIT MUSIC

The intense creativity of the band's work since early 1999 had one more outlet, a mini-album called *I Might Be Wrong: Live Recordings*, released at the end of 2001. Almost entirely consisting of songs from *Kid A* and *Amnesiac* (and the third released version of 'Morning Bell' in under two years), it was, on the face of it, an oddly conventional step. Live albums are traditionally a ruse for bands to buy themselves time for rest and recuperation, without the ominous finality that a 'greatest hits' package can imply.

But Radiohead, as ever, ring the changes. Most live albums are (or pretend to be) continuous recordings of a single concert. *I Might Be Wrong* is a selection of isolated tracks, shorn of context, avoiding any notion of a communal experience. What it does offer, however, is the songs from the last few years, devoid of studio inventiveness, and allowed to breathe. It's proof that, however avant-garde and experimental they were getting, Radiohead still knew how to knuckle down to the tough task of writing good songs. Tracks that had relied on electronic effects or extra musicians had to find their power elsewhere. For example, the horn-driven 'The National Anthem' is here ushered in with a gentle injection of vocal percussion.

Thom Yorke as human beatbox? Is there no end to the man's talents? In their live, stripped-down state, tracks such as 'Like Spinning Plates' also reveal something that might have been forgotten - Thom's abilities as one of the most emotionally lacerating singers currently working in the rock business.

The real treat in *I Might Be Wrong* for devoted fans is the first official release of 'True Love Waits'. The song had been an in-concert favourite for some years, and its yearning helplessness forms a lyrical thread as far back as 'Creep'. Obviously, it's not just a bog-standard love song - Thom vows to "dress like your niece and wash your swollen feet" - but the yearning coda of "just don't leave" is as direct a declaration of love as any singer has made.

The reviews tended to see the new, pared-down versions of the songs as a relief from the self-conscious art rock of the studio. Stephen Dalton argued in *Uncut*: "Radiohead prove here that they can conjure blazing intensity, visceral physicality and raging rock dynamics from even wilfully opaque jazzoid chuffing." "Put simply," wrote Ted Kessler in the *NME*, "*I Might Be Wrong* sounds significantly better than both of the studio albums that spawned it." While that might have been slightly excessive, the critical consensus was that this was a refreshing take on a selection of songs that had been subject to intensive analysis in recent months. Not the third part of a trilogy, then, but a fascinating appendix to one of the most courageous experiments in modern music.

And, as 'True Love Waits' fades out, we've come full circle. The band that first hit paydirt with a sad song about unrequited love rewrite the whole users' manual to rock 'n' roll then realise it's all about love songs in the end. But the journey has been more than worthwhile.

What's on the horizon for the band? Although there have been occasional side projects and collaborations, Radiohead have kept the same line-up intact for over a decade. There's a temptation in some quarters to see them as a reluctant voice of a generation, plus four other blokes, but the reality is more complex than that. Granted, Thom Yorke has staked his claim to being one of the most important singers and lyricists in rock history, as well as proving to be a responsible figurehead for communicating social and political messages to a disaffected fan base. Jonny Greenwood is simply one of the most passionate, imaginative and technically gifted rock guitarists of all time. However, the music proves that the sum of Radiohead will always be greater than its constituent parts. With the assistance of Nigel Godrich, the unofficial sixth member, the sheer density of ideas that Thom, Jonny, Ed, Colin and Phil can cram onto a single album is simply breathtaking. Any full-blown solo projects will be of interest, but it's likely they'll remain in the shadow of one of the most consistent bodies of work to be found in popular music.

It's this consistency that makes them stand out. Of course, there are other bands with the guts and imagination to break away from the norms of musical convention. The post-techno grooves of Richard D James (aka the Aphex Twin) and the sumptuous prog intensity of the Telstar Ponies are two avenues that should interest any fans impatient for new Radiohead product. And of course there are acts perceived to be influenced by Radiohead, like their Oxford neighbours Rock Of Travolta (described in *Careless Talk* as what might happen "if Belle and Sebastian had listened to Black Sabbath"), and the snarling Mogwai. But only Radiohead have managed to sell millions of records and hundreds of thousands of concert tickets across the globe, and still maintain their critical standing and integrity.

Of course, nothing is certain, and perspectives change. Thom has admitted that fatherhood (Noah was born in early 2001) has relaxed him a little. As he told Craig McLean in *The Face*, 'A friend said, when he found out Rachel and I were having a baby, 'Thank fuck for that. Maybe you'll stop throwing your rattle out of your pram.'" Maybe family life will start to dilute the intense camaraderie between the five band members.

Whatever happens next, Radiohead have created music without the accepted furniture of rock 'n' roll - the riff, the hook, the chorus, the guitar solo - and made it both credible and commercially successful. For the first time since The Beatles, a band has redefined what popular music is and can be. It's probably too early to make any claims about their historical importance - apart from anything else, they're still working, still recording, still pushing back the boundaries of sound.

Or maybe they're just discovering that, for some people, there aren't any boundaries.

# CHAPTER 12

DISCOGRAPHY

# DISCOGRAPHY

## ALBUMS

**Pablo Honey** - *You / Creep / How Do You? / Stop Whispering / Thinking About You / Anyone Can Play Guitar / Ripcord / Vegetable / Prove Yourself / I Can't / Lurgee / Blow Out.* US Version added *Creep (Radio Edit).* Japanese Version added *Pop Is Dead / Inside My Head / Million Dollar Question / Creep (Live) / Ripcord (Live)*
CD, LP, Cassette - Parlophone 1993

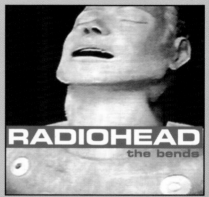

**The Bends** - *Planet Telex / The Bends / High And Dry / Fake Plastic Trees / Bones / (Nice Dream) / Just / My Iron Lung / Bullet Proof... I Wish I Was / Black Star / Sulk / Street Spirit (Fade Out).* Japanese Version added *How Can You Be Sure? / Killer Cars*
CD, LP, Cassette, Minidisc - Parlophone 1995

**OK Computer** - *Airbag / Paranoid Android / Subterranean Homesick Alien / Exit Music (For A Film) / Let Down / Karma Police / Fitter Happier / Electioneering / Climbing Up The Walls / No Surprises / Lucky / The Tourist.* (Some CDs, bearing the 1-6-11-NL number, play Pink Floyd's *Dark Side Of The Moon* album instead)
CD, LP, Cassette, Minidisc - Parlophone 1997

**Kid A** - *Everything In Its Right Place / Kid A / The National Anthem / How To Disappear Completely / Treefingers / Optimistic / In Limbo / Idioteque / Morning Bell / Motion Picture Soundtrack*
CD, LP, Cassette, Minidisc, 10" Vinyl - Parlophone 2000

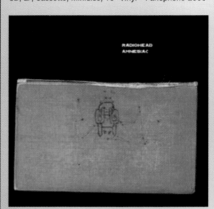

**Amnesiac** - *Packt Like Sardines In A Crushd Tin Box / Pyramid Song / Pulk/Pull Revolving Doors / You And Whose Army? / I Might Be Wrong / Knives Out / Morning Bell / Amnesiac / Dollars And Cents / Hunting Bears / Like Spinning Plates / Life In A Glasshouse*
CD, LP, Cassette, Minidisc - Parlophone 2001

## MINI-ALBUMS

**Itch** - *Stop Whispering (US Version) / Thinking About You / Faithless, The Wonder Boy / Banana Co. / Killer Cars (Live) / Vegetable (Live) / You (Live) / Creep (Live)*
CD - Toshiba (Japan) 1994

**Airbag/How Am I Driving?** - *Airbag / Melatonin / Pearly\* / A Reminder / Polyethylene (Parts 1 & 2) / Palo Alto / Meeting In The Aisle*
CD - Capitol (USA & Canada) 1998

**I Might Be Wrong: Live Recordings** - *National Anthem / I Might Be Wrong / Morning Bell / Like Spinning Plates / Idioteque / Everything In Its Right Place / Dollars And Cents / True Love Waits*
CD, LP - Parlophone 2001

## SINGLES/EPs

**Hometown Atrocities EP** - *I Don't Want To Go To Woodstock* - Headless Chickens Featuring Thom Yorke
7" Vinyl - Hometown Atrocities 1989

**On A Friday** - *What Is That You Say? / Stop Whispering / Give It Up* - On A Friday
Cassette - 1991

**Manic Hedgehog Demos** - *I Can't / Nothing Touches Me / Thinking About You / Phillipa Chicken / You* - On A Friday
Cassette - 1991

**Drill** - *Prove Yourself / Stupid Car / You / Thinking About You*
CD, 7" Vinyl, Cassette - Parlophone 1992

**Creep** - *Creep / Lurgee / Inside My Head / Million $ Question*
CD, 12" Vinyl, Cassette - Parlophone 1992

**Anyone Can Play Guitar** - *Anyone Can Play Guitar / Faithless, The Wonder Boy / Coke Babies*
CD, 12" Vinyl, Cassette - Parlophone 1993

**Anyone Can Play Guitar** - *Anyone Can Play Guitar*
LP, CD, Cassette - Parlophone 1993

**Anyone Can Play Guitar** - *Anyone Can Play Guitar / Creep / Pop Is Dead / Thinking About You (Killer Cars) / Killer Cars (Acoustic, Live)* - Australian Tour Souvenir
CD Digipack - Parlophone (Australia) 1994

**Pop Is Dead** - *Pop Is Dead / Banana Co. (Acoustic) / Creep (Live) / Ripcord (Live)*
CD, 12" Vinyl, Cassette - Parlophone 1993

**Creep** - *Creep / The Bends (Live) / Prove Yourself (Live) / Creep (Live)* - Black Sessions
CD - Parlophone (France) 1993

**Creep [Promo]** - *Creep*
CD - Capitol 1993

**Creep** - *Creep / Yes I Am / Inside My Head (Live At The Metro) / Creep (Acoustic)*
CD - Parlophone (Netherlands) 1993

**Creep** - *Creep / Yes I Am / Blow Out (Phil Vinall Remix) / Inside My Head (Live At The Metro)*
CD, 7" Vinyl, Cassette - Parlophone 1993

**Creep** - *Creep (Acoustic) / You (Live) / Vegetable (Live) / Killer Cars (Live)*
12" Vinyl - Parlophone 1993

**Creep [Promo]** - *Creep (Acoustic At Kroq, La)*
CD - Capitol 1993

**Creep** - *Creep / Faithless, The Wonder Boy*
7" - Capitol 1993

**Creep [Promo]** - *Creep (Edit Clean Version) / Creep (Album Version)*
CD - Capitol 1993

**Jukebox Green Vinyl [Promo]** - *Creep / Anyone Can Play Guitar*
Jukebox 7" Vinyl - Capitol 1993

**Pop Is Dead** - *Pop Is Dead / Banana Co. (Acoustic) / Creep (Live) / Ripcord (Live)*
12", CD, Cassette - Parlophone 1993

**Stop Whispering [US CD1]** - *Stop Whispering (US Version - Chris Sheldon Remix) / Creep (Acoustic) / Pop Is Dead / Inside My Head (Live)*
CD - Capitol (USA) 1993

**Stop Whispering [US CD2]** - *Stop Whispering (US Version) / Prove Yourself / Lurgee*
CD - Capitol 1993

**Stop Whispering [Promo]** - *Ripcord / Prove Yourself / Faithless, The Wonder Boy / Stop Whispering*
12" - Parlophone 1993

**Stop Whispering [Promo]** - *Stop Whispering (US Version) / Stop Whispering (LP Version)*
CD - Capitol 1993

**My Iron Lung** - *My Iron Lung / The Trickster / Punchdrunk Lovesick Singalong / Lozenge Of Love*
CD, 12" Vinyl - Parlophone 1994

**My Iron Lung** - *My Iron Lung / Lewis (Mistreated) / Permanent Daylight / You Never Wash Up After Yourself*
CD, Vinyl - Parlophone 1994

**My Iron Lung** - *My Iron Lung / The Trickster / Lewis (Mistreated) / Punchdrunk Lovesick Singalong*
12", Cassette - Parlophone 1994

**Australian EP** - *My Iron Lung / The Trickster / Lewis (Mistreated) / Punchdrunk Lovesick Singalong / Permanent Daylight / Lozenge Of Love / You Never Wash Up After Yourself / Creep (Acoustic)*
CD - EMI Int. 1998

**My Iron Lung** - *My Iron Lung / The Trickster / Lewis (Mistreated) / Permanent Daylight / You Never Wash Up After Yourself*
CD - Parlophone (Netherlands) 1994

**My Iron Lung** - *My Iron Lung / The Trickster / Punchdrunk Lovesick Singalong / Lewis (Mistreated) / Permanent Daylight / You Never Wash Up After Yourself*
CD - Capitol 1994

**My Iron Lung** - *My Iron Lung / Permanent Daylight / Banana Co. / My Iron Lung (Live)*
CD - Parlophone (Netherlands) 1994

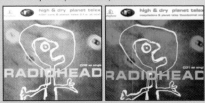

**High And Dry** - *High And Dry / Planet Telex / Maquiladora / Planet Telex (Steve Osborne Hexadecimal Mix)*
CD - Parlophone 1995

**High And Dry** - *High And Dry / Planet Telex / Killer Cars / Planet Telex (LFO Mix)*
CD - Parlophone 1995

**High And Dry** - *High And Dry / India Rubber / Maquiladora / How Can You Be Sure? / Just (Live)*
CD - Capitol 1996

**High And Dry** - *High And Dry / Planet Telex / Maquiladora / Killer Cars*
CD - EMI 1995

**High And Dry [Promo]** - *High And Dry*
CD - Capitol 1995

**High And Dry** - *High And Dry / Planet Telex*
Cassette - Parlophone (Netherlands) 1995

**High And Dry** - *High And Dry / Planet Telex / Black Star*
7" - Capitol 1995

**Planet Telex** - *Planet Telex / Planet Telex (Osborn Mix) / Planet Telex (Mo-Wax Mix) / High And Dry*
12" Parlophone 1995

**Planet Telex** - *Planet Telex (Steve Osborne Hexadecimal Mix) / Planet Telex (LFO JD Mix) / Planet Telex (Steve Osborne Hexadecimal Dub) / High And Dry*
12" Vinyl - Parlophone 1995

**Planet Telex Club Mix DJ** - *Planet Telex (Album Version) / Planet Telex (Steve Osborne Hexadecimal Mix) / Planet Telex (LFO JD Mix) / Planet Telex (Alien Beatfreak Trashed Mix)*
12" Vinyl - Parlophone 1995

**High And Dry Live Package** - *High And Dry / Creep (Live) / My Iron Lung (Live) / Stop Whispering (Live) / Punchdrunk Lovesick Singalong (Live)*
CD - Parlophone (Netherlands) 1995

**Fake Plastic Trees** - *Fake Plastic Trees / India Rubber / How Can You Be Sure?*
CD, 12", Cassette - Parlophone 1995

**Fake Plastic Trees** - *Fake Plastic Trees / Fake Plastic Trees (Acoustic) / Bullet Proof... I Wish I Was (Acoustic) / Street Spirit (Fade Out) (Acoustic)*
CD - Parlophone 1995

**Fake Plastic Trees** - *Fake Plastic Trees / Planet Telex (Hexidecimal Mix) / Killer Cars / Fake Plastic Trees (Acoustic)*
CD - Capitol 1995

**Fake Plastic Trees** - *Fake Plastic Trees / India Rubber / How Can You Be Sure? / Fake Plastic Trees (Acoustic)*
CD - Parlophone (Netherlands) 1995

**Fake Plastic Trees [Promo]** - *Fake Plastic Trees / Fake Plastic Trees (Edit)*
CD - Parlophone 1995

**Fake Plastic Trees [Jukebox Promo]** - *Fake Plastic Trees / The Bends*
7" Vinyl - Capitol 1995

**Just** - *Just / Planet Telex (Karma Sunra Mix) / Killer Cars (Mogadon Version)*
CD, 12", Cassette - Parlophone 1995

Just - *Just / Bones (Live) / Planet Telex (Live) / Anyone Can Play Guitar (Live)*
CD - Parlophone 1995

Just [French Promo] - *Just*
CD - Parlophone 1995

Just [UK Promo] - *Just / Just (Edit)*
CD - Parlophone 1995

Just For College [Promo] - *Just / India Rubber / Maquiladora / How Can You Be Sure? / Just (Live)*
CD - Parlophone 1996

Just - *Just / Bones (Live) / Planet Telex (Karma Sunra Mix) / Killer Cars (Modagon Version)*
CD - Parlophone (Netherlands) 1996

Just - *Just / Bones (Live)*
Casette - Parlophone (Australia) 1996

Creep - *Creep / The Bends*
CD - Parlophone (France) 1996

Creep - *Creep / Killer Cars (Live At The Metro)*
CD - Parlophone (Netherlands) 1996

Bones - *Bones / Black Star*
CD - EMI (Belgium) 1996

Lucky - *Lucky / Meeting In The Aisle / Climbing Up The Walls (Fila Brazillia Mix)*
CD - Parlophone (France) 1998

Lucky [Promo] - *Lucky*
CD - Parlophone 1998

Street Spirit (Fade Out) - *Street Spirit (Fade Out) / Talk Show Host / Bishop's Robes*
CD - Parlophone 1996

Street Spirit (Fade Out) - *Street Spirit (Fade Out) / Banana Co. / Molasses*
CD - Parlophone 1996

Street Spirit (Fade Out) - *Street Spirit (Fade Out) / Bishop's Robes*
7" - Parlophone 1996

Street Spirit (Fade Out) - *Street Spirit (Fade Out) / Bishop's Robes / Talk Show Host / Molasses*
CD - Parlophone (Netherlands/Australia) 1996

Street Spirit (Fade Out) - *Street Spirit (Fade Out) / Anyone Can Play Guitar (Live) / Bones (Live) / Street Spirit (Fade Out) (Live)*
CD Parlophone (Netherlands) 1996

Street Spirit (Fade Out) [DJ Promo] - *Street Spirit (Fade Out) / Talk Show Host / Bishop's Robes*
12", 7" - Parlophone 1996

Street Spirit (Fade Out) [Promo] - *Street Spirit (Fade Out)*
CD - Parlophone 1996

The Bends - *The Bends / My Iron Lung (Live) / Bones (Live)* - The Irish release of this single plays *Planet Telex* rather than *The Bends*
CD - Parlophone 1996

Live EP (The Pinkpop Single) - *Fake Plastic Trees (Live) / Blow Out (Live) / Bones (Live) / You (Live) / High And Dry (Live)*
CD - Parlophone (Netherlands) 1996

Paranoid Android - *Paranoid Android / Polyethylene (Parts 1 & 2) / Pearly\**
CD - Parlophone 1997

Paranoid Android - *Paranoid Android / A Reminder / Melatonin*
CD - Parlophone 1997

Paranoid Android - *Paranoid Android / Polyethylene (Parts 1 & 2)*
7" Vinyl - Parlophone 1997

Paranoid Android - *Paranoid Android / Polyethylene (Parts 1 And 2) / Pearly\* / Let Down*
CD - EMI (Japan) 1997

Paranoid Android [Promo] - *Paranoid Android*
CD Digipack Capitol 1997

Karma Police - *Karma Police / Meeting In The Aisle / Lull*
CD - Parlophone 1997

Karma Police - *Karma Police / Climbing Up The Walls (Zero 7 Mix) / Climbing Up The Walls (Fila Brazillia Mix)*
CD - Parlophone 1997

Karma Police - *Karma Police / Climbing Up The Walls (Zero 7 Mix) / Meeting In The Aisle*
12" Vinyl - Parlophone 1997

Karma Police - *Karma Police / A Reminder / Melatonin*
CD - Parlophone (Australia/Netherlands) 1997

Karma Police - *Karma Police / A Reminder / Melatonin / Let Down*
CD - EMI (Japan) 1997

Let Down - *Let Down / Karma Police*
7" Vinyl - Capitol 1997

College Karma EP [Promo] - *Karma Police / Polyethylene (Parts 1 And 2) / Pearly\* / A Reminder / Melatonin / Paranoid Android*
CD Digipack - Capitol 1998

Karma Police - *Karma Police / Let Down*
CD - Parlophone (France) 1997

Karma Police [UK Promo] - *Karma Police*
CD - Parlophone 1997

Karma Police - *Karma Police / Lull*
7" - Parlophone 1997

Karma Police [Promo] - *Karma Police / A Reminder*
CD - Parlophone (France/Belgium/Netherlands) 1997

Karma Police [Promo] - *Karma Police / Paranoid Android*
CD - Parlophone (France) 1997

No Surprises - *No Surprises / Pearly\* (Remix) / Melatonin / Meeting In The Aisle / Bishop's Robes / A Reminder*
CD Digipack - Toshiba (Japan) 1997

No Surprises [UK CD1] - *No Surprises / Palo Alto / How I Made My Millions*
CD, Cassette - Parlophone 1998

No Surprises [UK CD2] - *No Surprises / Airbag (Live) / Lucky (Live)*
CD - Parlophone 1998

No Surprises - *No Surprises / Palo Alto*
12", 7" Vinyl - Parlophone 1998

No Surprises - *No Surprises / Meeting In The Aisle / Lull*
CD - Parlophone (Netherlands) 1998

No Surprises - *No Surprises / Palo Alto / How I Made My Millions / Airbag (Live In Berlin)*
CD - Parlophone (Australia) 1998

No Surprises [UK Promo] - *No Surprises*
CD - Parlophone 1998

Climbing Up The Walls [Promo] - *Climbing Up The Walls / Climbing Up The Walls (Fila Brazillia Mix) / Climbing Up The Walls (Zero 7 Mix)*
12" - Parlophone 1998

Let Down - *Let Down*
CD Digipack - Capitol 1998

Let Down - *Let Down / Parnoid Android / Exit Music (For A Film) / Electioneering / No Surprises / Airbag*
CD - EMI (Japan) 1998

Optimistic [Promo] - *Optimistic*
CD - Capitol 2000 and Parlophone 2000

The National Anthem [Promo] - *The National Anthem*
CD - Parlophone (Belgium) 2000

Idioteque [Promo] - *Idioteque*
CD, 12" - Parlophone 2000

How To Disappear Completely [Promo] - *How To Disappear Completely*
CD - Parlophone / Universal Music Poland 2000

Kid A - *Kid A*
CD - Parlophone 2000

Pyramid Song - *Pyramid Song / The Amazing Sounds Of Orgy / Trans-Atlantic Drawl*
CD - Parlophone 2001

Pyramid Song - *Pyramid Song / Fast-Track / Kinetic*
CD - Parlophone 2001

Pyramid Song - *Pyramid Song / Fast-Track / The Amazing Sounds Of Orgy*
12" Vinyl - Parlophone 2001

Pyramid Song - *Pyramid Song / Fast-Track / The Amazing Sounds Of Orgy / Trans-Atlantic Drawl / Kinetic*
CD - EMI (Japan) 2001

Pyramid Song - *Pyramid Song*
CD - Parlophone 2001

Pyramid Song [Pinkpop Single] - *Pyramid Song / The National Anthem (Live In Dublin) / Idioteque (Live In Dublin) / The National Anthem (Enhanced Video) / Idioteque (Enhanced Video)*
CD - Parlophone (Netherlands) 2001

Pyramid Song [Promo] - *Pyramid Song / I Might Be Wrong / Packt Like Sardines In A Crushd Tin Box / Dollars And Cents*
CD - Parlophone 2001

Pyramid Song - *Pyramid Song / Fast Track*
CD - Parlophone 2001

Knives Out - *Knives Out / Cuttooth / Life In A Glass House (Full Length)*
CD, 12" - Parlophone 2001

Knives Out - *Knives Out / Worrywort / Fog*
CD - Parlophone 2001

Knives Out - *Knives Out / Cuttooth / Life In A Glass House (Full Length) / Pyramid Song*
12" Vinyl - Parlophone 2001

Knives Out [UK CD1] - *Knives Out / Worrywort / Fog / Life In A Glass House (Full Length Version)*
CD - Parlophone 2001

Knives Out [UK CD2] - *Knives Out / Cuttooth / Life In A Glass House (Full Length Version) / Knives Out (Video)*
CD - Parlophone 2001

Knives Out [Promo] - *Knives Out*
CD - Capitol 2001

I Might Be Wrong [Promo] - *I Might Be Wrong*
CD - Capitol 2001

## COMPILATIONS

Volume 7 - *Stupid Car (Tinnitus mix)*
CD - Volume 1993.

Volume 13 - *(Nice Dream) (Demo)*
CD - Volume 1995

This Is Fort Apache - *Anyone Can Play Guitar*
CD - MCA 1995

Sharks Patrol These Waters - *Stupid Car (Tinnitus mix)*
CD - Volume 1995

Help! - *Lucky*
CD - Go! Discs 1995

Evening Session Priority Tunes - *Just (Session)*
CD - Virgin 1996

Vol. 1 - MTV Buzz Bin - *Creep*
CD - Universal/Mammoth 1997

Grammy Nominees 2001 - *Optimistic*
CD - Capitol 2001

## SOUNDTRACKS

SFW - *Creep*
CD - A&M 1994

Clueless - *Fake Plastic Trees (Acoustic)*
CD - Capitol 1995

William Shakespeare's Romeo And Juliet - *Talk Show Host (Nellee Hooper mix)*
CD - Premier 1996

Nowhere - *How Can You Be Sure?*
CD - Polygram 1997

Memento - *Treefingers*
CD - Thrive 2001

Vanilla Sky - *Everything In Its Right Place*
CD - Geffen 2001

## GUEST APPEARANCES

Come Again - *Wish You Were Here (Thom with Sparklehorse)*
CD - EMI 1997

White Magic For Lovers - *El President (Thom)* - Drugstore
CD - Roadrunner 1998

Psyence Fiction - *Rabbit In Your Headlights (Thom with DJ Shadow)* - UNKLE
CD, LP - A&M 1998

Velvet Goldmine OST - *2HB / Ladytron / Baby's On Fire / Bitter-Sweet / Tumbling Down (Thom and Jonny with Venus In Furs)*
CD - London 1999

Terror Twilight - *Platform Blues / Billie (Jonny)* - Pavement
CD, LP - Domino 1999

Stories From The City, Stories From The Sea - *One Line / Beautiful Feeling / This Mess We're In (Thom)* - PJ Harvey
CD - Island 2000

Dancer In The Dark OST - *I've Seen It All (Thom)* - Bjork
CD - Elektra 2000

7 Worlds Collide - *Paradise* - Neil Finn & Friends
CD, DVD - Parlophone 2001

## TRIBUTE ALBUMS

Electronic - *Paranoid Android (Luxury Harrison remix)* [Mitchell Sigman] / *Kid A* [George Sarah] / *Exit Music (For A Film)* [Motor Industries] / *High And Dry* [Transient] / *Idioteque* [In One Ear Out The Analog] / *Let Down* [Mitchell Sigman] / *Creep* [Galactic Achievement Society] / *Motion Picture Soundtrack* [In One Ear Out The Analog] / *Climbing Up The Walls* [Motor Industries] / *Fake Plastic Trees* [Transient] / *Everything In Its Right Place* [In One Ear Out The Analog] / *Filter Happiness* [Motor Industries] - Plastic Mutations
CD - Vitamin 2001

Anyone Can Play Radiohead - *Fitter Happier* [Silent Gray] / *No Surprises* [Paige] / *Creep* [Aleister Einstein] / *Fake Plastic Trees* [October Hill] / *Stop Whispering* [Dotfash] / *Exit Music (For A Film)* [Miranda Sex Garden] / *Planet Telex* [Secret Society] / *Karma Police* [Dragon Style] / *Climbing Up The Walls* [Diya Destruction] / *Everything In Its Right Place* [Meegs] / *Subterranean Homesick Alien* [The Iluminati] / *Bullet Proof..I Wish I Was* [PM Project] / *How To Disappear Completely* [Lunasect]
CD - Anagram 2001

Strung Out On OK Computer - The String Quartet Tribute To Radiohead - *Airbag / Paranoid Android / Subterranean Homesick Alien / Exit Music (For A Film) / Let Down / Karma Police / Fitter Happier / Electioneering / Climbing Up The Walls / No Surprises / Lucky / The Tourist* CD - Vitamin 2001

## BOOTLEGS

"For those of you with a tape-recorder, that was 'In Limbo'. I wouldn't want you to get it wrong."
(Thom's on-stage message to bootleggers, Arles, June 2000)

Bootlegs are unofficial releases of mixes, live recordings, downloads and rare tracks. There are numerous such items around featuring Radiohead and below are a selection of the most common ones. It should be noted that to sell or trade in bootleg material is a criminal offence, therefore they are only available from underground sources such as market stalls and record fairs. The authors and publishers of the book do not endorse any trade in such items nor do they have any further information about their availability.

## AUDIO BOOTLEGS

**Oxford Angels (Non-Album Tracks & Rarities Part 1)** - *Prove Yourself / Stupid Car / You / Thinking About You* [Tracks 1-4: "Drill" EP] / *Inside My Head / Million Dollar Question* [Tracks 5-6: "Creep" CD Single] / *Faithless, The Wonderboy / Coke Babies* [Tracks 7-8: "Anyone Can Play Guitar" CD Single] / *Pop Is Dead / Banana Co. (Acoustic)* [Tracks 9-10: "Pop Is Dead" CD Single] / *Creep (Acoustic) / Yes I Am* [Tracks 11-12: "Creep" CD Single] / *The Trickster / Lewis (Mistreated) / Punchdrunk Lovesick Singalong / Permanent Daylight / Lozenge Of Love / You Never Wash Up After You* [Tracks 13-18: "My Iron Lung" EP] / *Maquilladora / Killer Cars* [Tracks 19-20: "High & Dry" CD Single] / *India Rubber / How Can You Be Sure? / Molasses* [Tracks 21-23: "Fake Plastic Trees" CD Single]

**Paragons Of Virtue (Non-Album Tracks & Rarities Part 2)** - *Talk Show Host / Bishop's Robes* [Tracks 1-2: "Street Spirit" (Fade Out) CD Single 1] / *Banana Co. (Full Band Electric Version)* ["Street Spirit (Fade Out) CD Single 2] / *Polyethylene (Parts 1 & 2) / Pearly* [Tracks 4-5: "Paranoid Android" CD Single 1] / *A Reminder / Melatonin* [Tracks 6-7: "Paranoid Android" CD Single 2] / *Meeting In The Aisle / Lull* [Tracks 8-9: "Karma Police" CD Single 1] / *Climbing Up The Walls (Zero 7 Mix) / Climbing Up The Wall (Fila Brazilla Mix)* [Tracks 10-11: "Karma Police" CD Single 2] / *Palo Alto / How I Made My Millions* [Tracks 12-13: "No Surprises" CD Single 1] / *Airbag (Live In Berlin) / Lucky (Live In Florence)* ["No Surprises" CD Single 2] / *Fake Plastic Trees (Acoustic)* ["Clueless" Soundtrack Album] / *Wonderwall* [Rare Version Of Oasis' Cover] / *My Iron Lung (Live At The Forum)* ["The Bends" Import CD Single] / *Creep (Live In Amsterdam)* ["High & Dry" Import CD Single]

**Creepshow (LA 1993)** - *You / The Bends / Vegetable / Creep / Ripcord / Stop Whispering / Pop Is Dead / Thinking About You / Faithless, The Wonderboy / Blow Out*

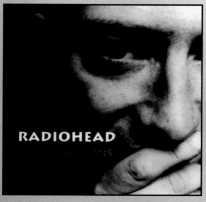

**Black Session (Covers, Live & Studio Sessions 1993-1995)** - *The Bends / Prove Yourself / Rhinestone Cowboy (Cover Version) / Stop Whispering / Anyone Can Play Guitar* [Black Session From Feb.23rd 1993] / *Hight And Dry / Fake Plastic Trees / Street Spirit / You / Planet Telex / Creep* [Black Session From Feb. 21st 1995] / *Introduction (A Capella) / Bones / You / Ripcord / Creep / My Iron Lung / Inside My Head* [Reading Festival 1994]

**Oxford Devils (B-Sides, Demos & Remixes 1993-1997)** - *Banana Co. / Talk Show Host / Bishop's Robes* [Tracks 1-3 "Street Spirit" B-Side] / *Polyethylene (Parts 1 & 2) / Pearly / A Reminder / Melatonin* [Tracks 4-7 "Paranoid Android" B-Side] / *Meeting In The Aisle / Lull* [Tracks 8-9 "Karma Police" B-Side] / *The Bends / Just / (Nice Dream)* [Tracks 10-12 - Demos] / *Stupid Car (Tinnitus Mix) / Stop Whispering (U.S. Remix) / Blow Out (Phil Vinnall Remix) / Killer Cars (Mogadon Version) / Talk Show Host (Nellee Hooper Remix) / Talk Show Host (Romeo & Juliet Reprise) / No Surprises* [Later With Jools Holland, May 1997] / *Electioneering* [Tonight With Jay Leno, September 1997] / *Nobody Does It Better* [MTV Europe, August 1997]

**Unplugged (1994-1996)** - *Killer Cars / Wonderwall / Blow Out / Street Spirit* [Tracks 1-4 CBS Studio, Canada 1996] / *Lucky / High And Dry / Motion Picture Soundtrack / Fake Plastic Trees* [Tracks 5-8 Rockville, USA 1996] / *Black Star / Street Spirit / Subterranean Homesick Alien* ["Johnny Walker Show", BBC Radio 1995] / *Thinking About You* ["T In The Park" Festival, Scotland 1996] / *Creep* [KROQ Studios, USA 1995] / *Just (Acoustic Demo) / Lozenge Of Love* [Live At The Forum, London 1995] / *Bullet Proof..I Wish I Was / Killer Cars / Banana Co. / Yes I Am* [Tracks 16-19 "On The Edge", USA 1994] / *Airbag / Fake Plastic Trees* [Tracks 20-21 KFM Studios, London 1995]

**Unplugged Vol. 2** - *You / Lucky / Subterranean Homesick Alien / Fake Plastic Trees / Street Spirit / Bullet Proof..I Wish I Was / Stop Whispering / Faithless, The Wonderboy / Ripcord / Pop Is Dead / Vegetable / The Bends / How Can You Be Sure / (Nice Dream) / Stupid Car / No Surprises / Paranoid Android / Exit Music / Talk Show Host*

**Electric Sessions (Radio And TV 1994-1997)** - *Paranoid Android* [Maida Vale Studios, London 1997] / *Exit Music* [Jo Whiley Show, BBC 1997] / *No Surprises / Airbag / Paranoid Android* [Tracks 3-5 Later With Jools Holland, 1997] / *Talk Show Host / Climbing Up The Walls / Exit Music / No Surprises* [Tracks 6-9 BBC Evening Session 1997] / *Electioneering* [Tonight Show, USA

1997] / *Just* [MTV Studios 1995] / *The Bends* [Later With Jools Holland, 1995] / *Anyone Can Play Guitar / Bones / Street Spirit* [Teww Meter Sessions, Holland 1995] / *Maquiladora* [BBC Evening Session 1994]

**Climbing Up The Walls** - *Paranoid Android* [The Evening Session] / *Polyethylene Parts 1 & 2* [UK B-Side] / *Pearly* [UK B-Side] / *No Surprises* [Later With Jools Holland] / *Airbag* [Later With Jools Holland] / *A Reminder* [UK B-Side] / *Melatonin* [UK B-Side] / *Talk Show Host* [The Evening Session] / *Climbing Up The Walls* [The Evening Session] / *Meeting In The Aisle* [UK B-Side] / *Lull* [UK B-Side] / *Climbing Up The Walls* [Zero 7 Mix] / *Exit Music (For A Film)* [The Evening Session] / *Climbing Up The Walls (Fila Brazilia Mix)* / *Paranoid Android* [Later With Jools Holland]

**England 1994, The Whisky, Hollywood USA 1993** - *You / Ripcord / Creep / My Iron Lung / Pop Is Dead / Stop Whispering / Anyone Can Play Guitar / You / The Bends / Vegetable / Creep / Ripcord / Stop Whispering / Pop Is Dead / Thinking About You / Faithless, The Wonder Boy / Blow Out*

**Airwaves (1995)** - *My Iron Lung / Bones / Anyone Can Play Guitar / High And Dry / Fake Plastic Trees / Planet Telex / Just / The Bends / Just / Anyone Can Play Guitar / Bones / High And Dry / Street Spirit (Fade Out) / Fake Plastic Trees / Planet Telex / My Iron Lung*

**The Warehouse (Toronto 1995)** - *The Bends / Bones / Bullet Proof / My Iron Lung / Prove Yourself / Street Spirit / Lucky / Creep / (Nice Dream) / High And Dry / Planet Telex / Anyone Can Play Guitar / Just / Blow Out / Fake Plastic Trees / Thinking About You / You / Black Star / Inside My Head*

**Planet Paradiso (Amsterdam, 1995)** - *The Bends / Bones / Bullet Proof..I Wish I Was / My Iron Lung / Lucky / Creep / Bishop's Robes / High And Dry / Planet Telex / Inside My Head / Just / Fake Plastic Trees / No Surprises / You / Black Star / (Nice Dream) / Stop Whispering*

**I Wanna Be Jim Morrison (Sapporo 1995)** - *My Iron Lung / Bones / Just / Black Star / You / The Bends / Street Spirit / High And Dry / (Nice Dream) / Killer Cars / Anyone Can Play Guitar / Fake Plastic Trees / Planet Telex / Faithless, The Wonder Boy / When I'm Like This (How Can You Be Sure?) / Stop Whispering*

**Painkiller (LA/Atlanta 1995)** - *The Bends / Just / Anyone Can Play Guitar / High And Dry / Planet Telex / Fake Plastic Trees / My Iron Lung / Creep / Stop Whispering / Street Spirit / Lucky / Bullet Proof..I Wish I Was / You / Subterranean Homesick Alien / Fake Plastic Trees / Nobody Does It Better / Creep*

**The Best Thing That You Ever Had (Boston 1996, Milton Keynes 1995)** - *My Iron Lung / Bones / High And Dry / Bullet Proof..I Wish I Was / Street Spirit (Fade Out) / Planet Telex / Stop Whispering / (Nice Dream) / Lucky /*

*Creep / Lurgee / Anyone Can Play Guitar / Just / Blow Out / Fake Plastic Trees / The Bends*

**Big Day Out (Galway 1996)** - *My Iron Lung / Bones / Bullet Proof..I Wish I Was / Planet Telex / Black Star / High And Dry / Lucky / (Nice Dream) / Creep / Anyone Can Play Guitar / Street Spirit (Fade Out) / Just / The Bends/Fake Plastic Trees / Street Spirit (Fade Out) / Just / Maquiladora*

**Live From Planet Earth, (Glasgow (T In The Park) 1996, Stockholm 1995)** - *My Iron Lung / Anyone Can Play Guitar / Bullet Proof..I Wish I Was / Planet Telex / High And Dry / Lucky / (Nice Dream) / Bones / Street Spirit (Fade Out) / The Bends / Just / Creep / Fake Plastic Trees / Thinking About You / Vegetable / Black Star / Creep / Stop Whispering*

**Fade Out (Milton Keynes 1995 + Bonus Tracks)** - *My Iron Lung / Bones / Anyone Can Play Guitar / High And Dry / Fake Plastic Trees / Planet Telex / Just / The Bends / Just / High And Dry / Street Spirit (Fade Out) / Fake Plastic Trees / Bullet Proof..I Wish I Was*

**The Outbends, Hollywood, Amsterdam 1995, Radio One Session 1996** - *The Bends / Just / Anyone Can Play Guitar / High And Dry / Planet Telex / Fake Plastic Trees / My Iron Lung / Creep / Stop Whispering / Creep / Street Spirit (Fade Out) / High And Dry / Fake Plastic Trees / Street Spirit (Fade Out) / My Iron Lung*

**Pop Is Dead (Stockholm 1995, Vancouver 1996, Holland 1995)** - *Bones / High And Dry / Lucky / Creep / Bishop's Robes / You / Fake Plastic Trees / Just / Street Spirit (Fade Out) / Star / (Nice Dream) / Stop Whispering / Street Spirit (Fade Out) / Killer Cars / Wonderwall / Blow Out / Subterranean Homesick Alien / My Iron Lung*

**Boston (1996)** - *My Iron Lung / Bones / High And Dry / Bullet Proof..I Wish I Was / Street Spirit / Planet Telex / Stop Whispering / (Nice Dream) / Lucky / Creep / Lurgee / Anyone Can Play Guitar / Just / Blow Out / Fake Plastic Trees / The Bends*

**Kill All - The Rarities Collection (1996)** - *Airbag / No Surprises / Paranoid Android* [Tracks 1-3: Later With Jools Holland, 1997] / *Talk Show Host (Remix)* ["Romeo And Juliet" Soundtrack, 1997] / *Wish You Were Here* [Pink Floyd Cover, Thom with Sparklehorse] / *Street Spirit (Thom Solo) / Killer Cars (Thom Solo) / Wonderwall* [Oasis Cover, Thom with Jon Auer and Ken Stringfellow of The Posies] *Street Spirit* [Tracks 6-8: Unplugged at CBS Studios, Canada 1996] / *Lucky / High And Dry / Fake Plastic Trees* [Tracks 9-11: Unplugged in Rockville, USA 1996] / *Subterranean Homesick Alien* [Unplugged From Johnny Walker Show, 1995] / *Creep* [Unplugged from "Creep" CD Single] / *Pop Is Dead* [From "Pop Is Dead CD Single] / *Climbing Up The Walls / Exit Music (For A Film)* [Tracks 15-16: Radio One's Evening Session, 1997]

**Fifth Element (Milan 1997)** - *Lucky / Airbag / Planet Telex / No Surprises / Fake Plastic Trees / Paranoid Android / Let Down / Karma Police / Subterranean Homesick Alien / The Bends / Creep / Street Spirit (Fade Out) / Thinking About You / High And Dry / The Tourist*

**Glastonbury 1997 (Plus Sessions)** - *Planet Telex / Exit Music / The Bends / (Nice Dream) / Paranoid Android / Karma Police / Creep / Climbing Up The Walls / No Surprises / Talk Show Host / Bones / Just / Airbag / No Surprises / Climbing Up The Walls*

**Alive Computer (Live Glastonbury 1997 & Rome 1995)** - *Paranoid Android / Karma Police / Creep / Climbing Up The Walls / No Surprises / Talk Show Host / My Iron Lung / Just / High And Dry / Street Spirit / The Vegetable / You / Prove Yourself / Planet Telex / Bullet Proof / Creep*

**Mists Of Avalon (Live at the Avalon Farm, London 1997)** - *Planet Telex / Exit Music / The Bends / Nice Dreams / Paranoid Android / Karma Police / Creep / Climbing Up The Walls / No Surprises / Talk Show Host / Bones / Just / Fake Plastic Trees / High And Dry / Street Spirit*

**Les Eurock Eennes (France 1997 + Studio Outtakes)** - *Lucky / Bones / Airbag / My Iron Lung / Exit Music (For A Film) / The Bends / No Surprises / Talk Show Host / Paranoid Android / Street Spirit / Creep / Just / Exit Music (For A Film) / Paranoid Android / Climbing Up The Walls*

**Computer KO (Utrecht 1997)** - *Lucky / My Iron Lung / Airbag / Exit Music (For A Film) / Planet Telex / Talk Show Host / Fake Plastic Trees / Paranoid Android / Karma Police / You / Climbing Up The Walls / No Surprises / Just / Street Spirit / The Bends / Thinking About You / The Tourist*

**Come To Daddy G (New York 1997)** - *Karma Police / The Bends / Exit Music (For A Film) / Subterranean Homesick Alien / My Iron Lung / No Surprises / Bones / Paranoid Android / Fake Plastic Trees / Street Spirit (Fade Out) / No Surprises*

**Ground Control To Major Thom (New York & Radio Sessions 1997)** - *Karma Police / The Bends / Exit Music (For A Film) / Subterranean Homesick Alien / My Iron Lungs / No Surprises / Bones / Paranoid Android / Fake Plastic Trees / Street Spirit / No Surprises / Talk Show Host / Climbing Up The Walls / Exit Music (For A Film) / Just / Nobody Does It Better*

**The Dust And The Screaming (Tokyo 1998)** - *Meeting In The Aisle / Airbag / Talk Show Host / Exit Music (For A Film) / Climbing Up The Walls / Just / Karma Police / Fake Plastic Trees / Pearly* / Killer Cars (Acoustic) / Paranoid Android / Lurgee / Black Star / No Surprises / My Iron Lung / Lucky / Big Ideas (Acoustic) / Subterranean Homesick Alien / The Bends / Street Spirit (Fade Out) / Planet Telex / Bullet Proof..I Wish I Was / (Nice Dream) / Bones / You / Let Down / The Tourist*

**Amnesty International Concert (Paris 1998)** - *Lucky / Karma Police / Exit Music (For A Film) / Talk Show Host / My Iron Lung / No Surprises / Fake Plastic Trees / Bones / Paranoid Android / Street Spirit (Fade Out)*

**Human Rights (Live at the Universal Declaration Of Human Rights, Paris 1998 + Reading Festival 1994)** - *Lucky / Karma Police / Exit Music (For A Film) / Talk Show Host / My Iron Lung / No Surprises / Fake Plastic Trees / Bones / Paranoid Android / Street Spirit / Inside My Head / Coke Babies / Just / Pop is Dead / Anyone Can Play Guitar*

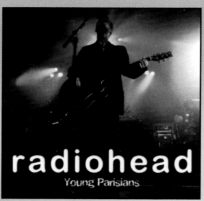

**Young Parisians (Live Paris 1999 + Bonus Tracks)** - *Lucky / Karma Police / Exit Music (For A Film) / Talk Show Host / My Iron Lung / No Surprises / Fake Plastic Trees / Bones / Paranoid Android / Just / The Bends / Killer Cars / Vegetable / You / Creep / Ripcord*

**Yes I Am (Various Acoustic Sessions 1999)** - *Creep / Fake Plastic Trees / Banana Co. / Airbag / Lucky / High And Dry / Motion Picture Soundtrack / Fake Plastic Trees / Black Star / Street Spirit / Subterranean Homesick Alien / Thinking About You / Creep / Just / Lozenge Of Love / Bullet Proof..I Wish I Was / Killer Cars / Banana Co. / Yes I Am*

**Kid Rocks (Glasgow 2000)** - *The National Anthem / Morning Bell / Lucky / My Iron Lung / In Limbo / Paranoid Android / Exit Music / You And Whose Army? / Climbing Up The Walls / Idioteque / Just / No Surprises / Dollars And Cents / Airbag / Everything In Its Right Place / I Might Be Wrong / Fake Plastic Trees / The Bends / How To Disappear Completely / Karma Police / The Tourist / Motion Picture Soundtrack*

Copenhagen 2000

**Copenhagen (Live in Copenhagen, DK 2000)** - *Morning Bell / Lucky / My Iron Lung / In Limbo Dedicated To The Moon / Fake Plastic Trees / You And Whose Army / Climbing Up The Walls / No Surprises / Dollars And Cents / Street Spirit / Airbag / Talk Show Host*

**Tivoli Experience (Barcelona 2000)** - *Talk Show Host / Bones / Optimistic / Karma Police / Morning Bell / How To Disappear Completely / Street Spirit / The National Anthem / My Iron Lung / No Surprises / Climbing Up The Walls / Lucky / Exit Music / Knives Out / Airbag / Everything In Its Right Place / Just / Egyptian Song / Lurgee / Paranoid Android*

**Dollars And Marks (Berlin/Paris 2000)** - *Optimistic / Morning Bell / Karma Police / The National Anthem / In Limbo / No Surprises / My Iron Lung / Dollars And Cents / Bishop's Robes / Talk Show Host / Kid A / You And Whose Army? / Airbag / Lucky / How To Disappear Completely / Paranoid Android / Everything In Its Right Place / Egyptian Song / Exit Music / Knives Out / Big Ideas / Nice Dream / Morning Bell / Idioteque*

**Copenhagen (2000)** - *The National Anthem / Lucky / My Iron Lung / In Limbo / Paranoid Android / Fake Plastic Trees / No Surprises / Dollars And Cents / Street Spirit (Fade Out) / Everything In Its Right Place*

**Kid's Birthday Party (Warrington 2000)** - *The National Anthem / Morning Bell / Karma Police / In Limbo / Paranoid Android / Permanent Daylight / Egyptian Song / Street Spirit / Climbing Up The Walls / Dollars & Cents / Lucky / Idioteque / Just / Everything In Its Right Place / Exit Music / The Thief*

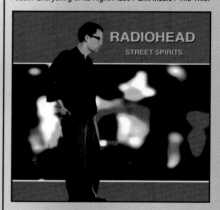

**Street Spirits (Toronto 2000)** - Disc 1 *National Anthem / Morning Bell / Airbag / In Limbo / Optimistic / Lucky / My Iron Lung / You And Whose Army / No Surprises / Dollars And Cents / Exit Music (For A Film) / Talk Show Host* - Disc 2 *How To Disappear Completely / Paranoid Android / Idioteque / Just / Everything In Its Right Place / I Might Be Wrong / Street Spirit / Follow Me Around / The Bends / Pyramid Song / Motion Picture Soundtrack / Karma Police*

**Karma In The Arena (Arles, France 2000)** - Disc 1 *Talk Show Host / Bones / Optimistic / Karma Police / Planet Telex / Morning Bell / Dollars And Cents / Street Spirit / National Anthem / My Iron Lung / No Surprises / Climbing Up The Walls* - Disc 2 *Lucky / Limbo / Exit Music / Air Bag / Everything In Its Right Place / Just / Knives Out / (Nice Dream) / Paranoid Android*

**Stop Coming On My F\*\*king MTV!**

Stop Coming On My F**Ing MTV! (Germany 2000) - Disc 1 *Optimistic / Talk Show Host / Karma Police / Morning Bell / You & Whose Army / National Anthem / My Iron Lung / In Limbo / No Surprises / Kid A / Dollars & Cents* - Disc 2 *Exit Music / F**Ing MTV! / Street Spirit / Climbing Up The Walls / Airbag / Everything In Its Right Place / How To Disappear / Lucky / Egyptian Song / Paranoid Android*

**RADIOHEAD LES ENFANTS TERRIBLE**

INCLUDES THE COMPLETE 'ON A FRIDAY' DEMO TAPE

Les Enfants Terrible (The Real Ultra Rare Trax Vol. 1) - *I Can't / Nothing Touches Me / Phillipa's Chicken / You* [Tracks 1-4 The Complete "On A Friday" Demo Tape] / *Sing A Song For You* [Cover Version Of A Tim Buckley Song] / *Union City Blue* [Cover Version Of A Blondie Song] / *How To Disappear Completely And Never Be Found (Live) / Big Ideas (Live) / I Promise (Live) / Lift (Live) / Man-O-War (Live) / Motion Picture Soundtrack (Demo Version) / True Love Waits (Live) / Thinking About You (Original EP Version) / Stop Whispering (US Version) / Paranoid Android* [Rare Live Version With Extended Keyboard Part]

**RADIOHEAD COUP D'ETAT**

ALSO FEATURING: MICHAEL STIPE, THE POSIES, ALANIS MORISSETTE

Coup D'Etat (The Real Ultra Rare Trax Vol. 2) - *Alligators In The New York Sewers (Live) / Lucky* [Live with Michael Stipe] / *Sunday Bloody Sunday (Live Cover Version) / Be Quiet And Drive (Live) / Creep (A Capella) / Everything In Its Right Place (Live) / Blow-Out* [Thom Yorke with The Posies, Live on US Radio] / *Rabbit In Your Headlights* [Thom Yorke & DJ Shadow] / *Big Boot (Live) / Fake Plastic Trees* [Alanis Morisette's Version] /

*Rhinestone Cowboy (Cover Version) / Morning Bell (Morning Bell) / El President* [With Thom guesting on Vocals] / *Ladytron* [From the 'Velvet Goldmine' movie] / *My Iron Lung (Re-Worked) / Video Killed The Radio Star (Cover Version)*

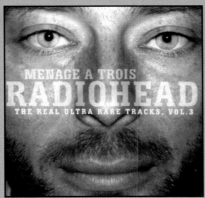

**MENAGE A TROIS RADIOHEAD THE REAL ULTRA RARE TRACKS, VOL.3**

Menage A Trois (The Real Ultra Rare Trax Vol. 3) - *I've Seen It All* [From "Dancing In The Dark" Soundtrack] / *Cowboy Song* [With Blur] / *Leave* [With Michael Stipe, from "Freedom For Tibet" concert] / *Let Down (Rare Mono Mix) / Egyptian Song / Wish You Were Here* [With Mark Linkous, from "Come Again"] / *Electioneering* [Live at Jay Leno Show 1997] / *Optimistic (Live) / Wonderwall* [The classic Oasis piss-take] / *Knives Out / Nobody Does It Better* [Cover Version of The 70's Bond theme] / *The Bends* [From Various Artists album "Long Live Tibet"] / *Bullet Proof..I Wish I Was (Acoustic) / You And Whose Army / Climbing Up The Walls (Fila Brazillia Mix) / Rock'n'roll Mcdonalds (Messing Around)*

Rock Am Ring (Nuremburg/Pinkpop, Netherlands 2001) - *The National Anthem / Morning Bell/ Lucky / Talk Show Host / In Limbo / My Iron Lung / Packt Like Sardines In A Crushd Tin Box / Exit Music (For A Film) / No Surprises / Dollars And Cents / Street Spirit / You And Whose Army? / Karma Police / I Might Be Wrong / Pyramid Song / Paranoid Android / Idioteque / Everything In Its Right Place / Airbag / Just / The Bends / How To Disappear Completely / Talk Show Host / In Limbo / My Iron Lung / Exit Music (For A Film) / No Surprises / Dollars And Cents*

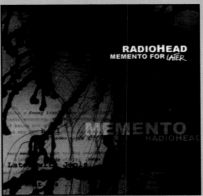

**RADIOHEAD MEMENTO FOR LATER**

**MEMENTO RADIOHEAD**

Memento For Later (Later With Jools Holland 2001) - *National Anthem / Morning Bell / Lucky / Packt Like Sardines In A Crushd Tin Box / No Surprises / Dollars And Cents / Life In A Glasshouse / Exit Music / I Might Be Wrong / Street Spirit / Paranoid Android / Idioteque / Everything In Its Right Place* / Bonus Tracks - *Karma Police / In Limbo / Paranoid Android / The Thief* [Live In Warrington, 2000]

**RADIOHEAD ∙ OXFORD ∙ JULY 7TH 2001 SOUTH PARK RADIOHEAD COMPLETE, LIVE & UNCUT**

South Park (Oxford 2001) - Disc 1 *National Anthem / Airbag / Morning Bell / Lucky / Packt Like Sardines In A Crushd Tin Box / My Iron Lung / Exit Music / Knives Out / No Surprises / Dollars And Cents / Street Spirit / I Might Be Wrong / Pyramid Song* - Disc 2 *Paranoid Android / Idioteque / Everything In Its Right Place / Karma Police / You And Whose Army? / How To Disappear Completely / Talk Show Host / The Bends / Creep*

## BOOTLEG VIDEO

San Diego 1993 - *You / Prove Yourself / The Bends / Vegetable / Creep / Lurgee / Ripcord / Faithless, The Wonderboy / Banana Co. / Stop Whispering / Inside My Head / Anyone Can Play Guitar / Pop Is Dead / Thinking About You / Blow Out*

La Luna, Brussels 1995 - *The Bends / Bones / Bullet Proof / My Iron Lung / Prove Yourself / Street Spirit / Lucky / Creep / (Nice Dream) / High And Dry / Planet Telex / Anyone Can Play Guitar / Just / Blow Out / Fake Plastic Trees / True Love Waits / You / Banana Co. / Nobody Does It Better / Inside My Head*

Glastonbury 1997 - *Lucky / My Iron Lung / Airbag / Planet Telex / Exit Music (For A Film) / The Bends / (Nice Dream) / Paranoid Android / Karma Police / Creep / Climbing Up The Walls / No Surprises / Talk Show Host / Bones / Just / Fake Plastic Trees / You / The Tourist / High And Dry / Street Spirit (Fade Out)*

San Francisco 1998 - *Meeting In The Aisle / Airbag / Planet Telex / Karma Police / Exit Music / Just / Banana Co. / Lucky / Paranoid Android / The Bends / (Nice Dream) / The Trickster / Climbing Up The Walls / No Surprises / Fake Plastic Trees / Bones / My Iron Lung / Big Ideas / Let Down / Street Spirit / Lurgee*

Philadephia 1998 - *Lucky / Lust / Airbag / Exit Music / Karma Police / Planet Telex / Electioneering / No Surprises / The Bends / Paranoid Android / Bones / (Nice Dream) / Lurgee / Talk Show Host / My Iron Lung / Fake Plastic Trees / Climbing Up The Walls / Creep / Polyethylene / Street Spirit*

## BOOKS & AUDIO BOOKS

*Radiohead: An Illustrated Biography* by Nick Johnstone
Paperback - Omnibus 1995

*The Bends (Sheet Music)*
Paperback - Warner Brothers 1995

*Radiohead: Green Plastic Wateringcan* by William Stone
Paperback - UFO 1996

*Radiohead: Coming Up For Air* by Steve Malins
Paperback - Virgin 1997

*OK Computer (Sheet Music)*
Paperback - International Music Publishing 1997

*Chatback Interview*
CD - Chatback 1997

*Pablo Honey (sheet music)*
Paperback - International Music Publishing 1998

*Radiohead Interview*
CD - Baktabak 1998

*Radiohead: The Interview*
CD - Talking Music 1998

*Jam With Radiohead: Guitar, Vocal Book And CD*
Paperback - Warner Brothers 1998

*Best Of Radiohead: Piano, Vocal, Guitar*
Paperback - Warner Brothers 1998

*Radiohead: From A Great Height* by Jonathan Hale
Paperback - ECW 1999

*Radiohead: Hysterical And Useless* by Martin Clarke
Paperback - Plexus 1999

*Star Profile*
CD - Mastertone 1999

*Maximum Radiohead*
CD - Chrome Dreams 2000

*Exit Music: The Radiohead Story* by Mac Randall
Paperback - Omnibus/Delta 2000

*Radiohead: Standing On The Edge* by Alex Ogg
Paperback - Boxtree 2000

*Radiohead X-Posed*
CD - Chrome Dreams 2001

*Radiohead* by Susan Black
Paperback - Omnibus 2002

*Radiohead: An Illustrated Biography* by Nick Johnstone
Paperback - Omnibus Press 1997

*Radiohead: Back to Save the Universe: The Stories behind Every Song* by James Doheny
Hardcover - Avalon New York - May 2002

There are also regular pieces about the band in publications such as *NME*, *Q*, *Uncut*, *The Wire* and *Careless Talk* (UK); *Rolling Stone*, *Spin*, *Alternative Press* and *Revolver* (USA). The official newsletter is *W.A.S.T.E.* (see www.waste.uk.com) and there are, unsurprisingly, dozens of fanzines devoted totally or in part to the music and activities of Abingdon's finest alumni.

## VIDEOS

**Radiohead - Astoria London** - *You / Bones / Ripcord / Black Star / Creep / The Bends / My Iron Lung / Prove Yourself / Maquiladora / Vegetable / Fake Plastic Trees / Just / Stop Whispering / Anyone Can Play Guitar / Street Spirit (Fade Out) / Pop Is Dead / Blow Out*
VHS - PMI 1996

**Radiohead - 7 Television Commercials** - *Paranoid Android / Street Spirit (Fade Out) / No Surprises / Just / High And Dry / Karma Police / Fake Plastic Trees*
VHS - PMI 1998

**Radiohead - Meeting People Is Easy**
VHS, DVD - Parlophone 1998

## RADIOHEAD ON THE WEB

For sourcing additional information about Radiohead, you really can't beat the World Wide Web. There are numerous sites about Radiohead containing a wide range of biographical information, pictures, up-to-the-minute news and tour dates as well as MP3's of both his well known and rarer tracks. The following sites are among the most comprehensive and a good place to start finding out about Radiohead online. Search engines such as Yahoo and Google can uncover many more fan sites. Up-to-date information can also be found on general music sites such as www.rollingstone.com, www.nme.com, www.mtv.com and www.getmusic.com.

www.radioheadfans.com

www.radiohead.com - The official site

www.followmearound.com

www.waste.uk.com - Radiohead merchandise and newsletter

www.greenplastic.com

www.myironduck.com

www.underworld.net/radiohead

www.fakeplasticcreep.homepad.com

www.thetourist.fsnet.co.uk
www.edskinkyshoelace.com - Fan site for a certain unfeasibly tall guitarist.
www.jonnygreenwood.net - Fan site for a shorter guitarist with good cheekbones.

www.soft.net.uk/kelly/rhead.htm - Karma karaoke - sing along with *OK Computer*. If you must.

www.slowlydownward.com - Site of Stanley Donwood, creator of the band's visual identity.

www.nologo.org - For fans and supporters of Naomi Klein and the ideas she expressed in No Logo.

www.zmag.org/chomsky - The best on-line guide to the works of Noam Chomsky.

## SUGGESTED LISTENING/READING

References for a few of the musicians, authors and ideas mentioned in the text.

**Albums**
Aphex Twin: *Drukqs* (Warp 2001)
Albert Ayler: *Live In Greenwich Village* (GRP 1998)
Beach Boys: *Pet Sounds* (Capitol 1966)
The Beatles: *The Beatles* (Apple 1968)
David Bowie: *The Rise And Fall Of Ziggy Stardust And The Spiders From Mars* (RCA 1972)
Ornette Coleman: *Something Else* (OJC 1958)
Elvis Costello And The Attractions: *Blood And Chocolate* (Demon 1996)
The Costello Show: *King Of America* (Demon 1986)
Miles Davis: *Bitches Brew* (Columbia 1969)
DJ Shadow: *Endtroducing…* (Mo' Wax 1996)
Bob Dylan: *Bringing It All Back Home* (CBS 1965)
Lunatic Calm: *Metropol* (BMG/V2 2001)
Humphrey Lyttleton: *Rent Party* (Stomp Off 1991)
Massive Attack: *Mezzanine* (Wild Bunch/Virgin 1998)
John Matthias: *Smalltown, Shining* (Lifelike 2001)
Mogwai: *Come On Die Young* (Chemikal Underground 1999)
Pink Floyd: *Wish You Were Here* (EMI 1975)
Pixies: *Death To The Pixies* (4AD 1997)
REM: *Automatic For The People* (Warner 1992)
Rock Of Travolta: *My Band's Better Than Yours* (Truck 2001)
Roxy Music: *Roxy Music* (Virgin 1972)
Shirehorses: *Our Kid Eh* (Columbia 2001)
Telstar Ponies: *Voices From The New Music* (Fire 1996)
The Unbelievable Truth: *Misc Music* (Shifty Disco 2001)

**Books**
Douglas Adams: *The Hitchhiker Trilogy* (Pan 1992)
Douglas Adams & Mark Carwardine: *Last Chance To See* (Pan 1991)
Noam Chomsky: *Profit Over People: Neoliberalism And Global Order* (Seven Stories 1998)
David Cogswell: *Chomsky For Beginners* (Writers And Readers 1993)
Matthew Collin: *This Is Serbia Calling* (Sepent's Tail 2001)
TS Eliot: *Collected Poems 1909-1962* (Faber 1974)
Naomi Klein: *No Logo* (Flamingo 2000)
Ani Pachen, Dalai Lama: *Sorrow Mountain* (Bantam 2001)
Craig Raine: *Collected Poems 1978-1998* (Picador 2000)
Walter Tevis: *The Man Who Fell To Earth* (Bloomsbury 1999)

# PHOTO CREDITS

Photos Courtesy of:
ALL ACTION, FAMOUS, REX, REDFERNS,

productions of record/CD artwork courtesy of Capital/Parlophone Records